EQUIPPING THE SAINTS

EQUIPPING THE SAINTS

Mobilizing Laity for Ministry

Edited by
Michael J. Christensen
with Carl E. Savage

Foreword by Leonard I. Sweet

ABINGDON PRESS
Nashville

EQUIPPING THE SAINTS: MOBILIZING LAITY FOR MINISTRY

This book is printed on recycled, acid-free paper.

Library of Congress Cataloging-in-Publication Data

Equipping the saints : mobilizing laity for ministry / edited by Michael J. Christensen with Carl E. Savage.
　　p.　cm.
Includes bibliographical references.
ISBN 0-687-02445-5 (alk. paper)
1. Lay ministry.　I. Christensen, Michael J.　II. Savage, Carl E.

BV677 .E64 2000
253—dc21

00-029967

00 01 02 03 04 05 06 07 08 09—10 9 8 7 6 5 4 3 2 1

MANUFACTURED IN THE UNITED STATES OF AMERICA

CONTENTS

FOREWORD 7
The Ministry of "Dedicated Servers"
Leonard I. Sweet

INTRODUCTION 11
Michael J. Christensen

CHAPTER ONE 17
Out of the Pew, into the World: Motivating for
Ministry
Jessica Farish Moffatt

CHAPTER TWO 39
The Loss and Recovery of Lay Ministry
Russell Moy

CHAPTER THREE 49
Life Together: Reclaiming the Ministry of Small Groups
Christine M. Anderson

CHAPTER FOUR 101
Team Building Through Spiritual Gifts
Brian K. Bauknight

CHAPTER FIVE 121
The Seeker Service in the Mainline Church
Eric Park

102421

CHAPTER SIX *142*
    Circuit Riding in the Twenty-First Century
        Robert Duncan Jr.

CHAPTER SEVEN *160*
    Three Streams, One River
      Michael J. Christensen

NOTES *185*

SELECTED BIBLIOGRAPHY ON MOBILIZING LAITY . . *193*
      Carl E. Savage

CONTRIBUTORS *203*

The Ministry of "Dedicated Servers"

Leonard I. Sweet

TheNextChurch has two next challenges: getting clear and clearing out. The first challenge is getting clear who Jesus is. The second challenge is clearing out spiritual deformities that dis-order the church's structural life and dis-able its mission.

This book picks up the second challenge and runs. But once seekers on The Way find that Jesus is The Truth, they experience The Life only insofar as they give their lives away as "dedicated servers" (another phrase the culture has stolen from the church). *Equipping the Saints* helps clear out obstacles that stand in the way of setting in motion the one doctrine that was introduced but not implemented during the Protestant Reformation: the "priesthood of all believers." As Martin Luther put it, "The fact is that our baptism consecrates us all without exception, and makes us all priests" (as quoted by Russell Moy in these pages).

One thing can be said with surety about Christianity in the twenty-first century: the role of pastoral leadership is dramatically shifting from representative to participatory models. Leadership involves less the doing of ministry than the dressing of the nonordained in the intellectual, spiritual, and outdoor outfits needed to minister in the world and become full ministerial partners with the ordained. Editor Michael Christensen employs Jesus' favorite water metaphor to express the book's organizing question: "How can ministerial leadership (clergy) move the people of God (laity) from the baptismal font into the full flow of ministry in the church and mission in the world?"

How we answer this question is critical to our future. What these authors call "NextChurch" is comprised of believers who insist on participating *in* ministry rather than finding fulfillment through supporting a representative ministry doing ministry *for* them. For us to reach the unchurched in the belly of the overchurched, we must learn to swim in what Christensen calls a "three streams, one river" philosophy of ministry: "In the New Reformation of the Laity, the people of God are rising up in opposition to clerical privilege, episcopal power, and ecclesial exclusivity in ministry." More than a metaphor for ministry, Christensen's "river vision" is a metaphor for living the whole of the Christian life.

We tend to forget that the Jesus movement was a lay mission. Jesus himself was a layman. He was born not of the tribe of Levi but of the tribe of David. According to Mosaic Law and the Levitical priesthood, Jesus could not be a priest. Some did call him "rabbi" or "teacher," but he was not educated formally in any rabbinical school, and received the same education accorded every layperson. When the layman Jesus proved to understand more of the Scriptures than the priests and religious authorities, the ensuing smears and sneers paved the path to Golgotha.

We tend to forget even more that the twelve disciples Jesus called to found his movement were all laypeople. Jesus had three years in which to save the world. How did he choose to spend those three years? Founding a megachurch? Launching a mass movement? Building a temple? Starting a new religion? He chose to spend what time he had training a small cell of disciples.

And how many priests or ordained rabbis were among the twelve Jesus chose? Not one. Emerito P. Nacpil, Resident Bishop Manila Area (Republic of the Philippines), assesses the character of Jesus' ministry as "a lay movement outside the religious establishment."[1] Professor Moy reframes the issue by abolishing the category of laity itself: Christianity got along fine for two hundred years without the laity, he writes. All were clergy.

Whether one abolishes the clergy or the laity, every spiritual awakening in Christian history has been in some fashion a rediscovery of this revolutionary characteristic of the Jesus movement. Brian K. Bauknight calls it the fundamental fact of church life: "There are sufficient spiritual gifts in every community of believers to do what God is calling that community to do in this particular moment of time." Unfortunately, most often the laity have been forced to make their own way in ministry and in the use of their spiritual gifts. In this essay and in his most recent book, Bauknight seeks to change that.

Another common characteristic of history's spiritual awakenings is the use of cutting-edge technologies. Robert Duncan Jr. shows how "the circuit rider of eighteenth-century American Methodism has become the cybersurfer of the twenty-first-century electronic frontier." Duncan's article is filled with practical ideas for how to integrate electronic technology in the life of the church, or as he puts it, how to "ride the circuit" in the church of the New Reformation. Christine M. Anderson's pioneering typology of "small groups" reveals why the best youth ministry is not one that has a pied piper youthworker and noisy programming, but one that disciples youth in cell communities and deploys youth in ministry with their families and friends.

While a ministry of all baptized believers is the stated understanding of ministry based on baptismal vows, most denominations still lift up ordination as the bar for ministry. Jessica Moffatt, who deftly explores the motivational mechanics of getting laity to see themselves as "ministers" (and those who can't as "dedicated servers" at least) asks a telling question: "We say that the ordained are 'set apart' for the ministry. Have we become so set apart that the laity do not feel a sense of their own ministry?" Even denominations like The United Methodist Church, which boasts a long history of lay ministry and a loud rhetoric of "the ministry of the baptized," are moving institutionally toward more exclusive understandings of "minister" as "one who has been ordained." This point is driven home by The United Methodist Church's professionalization of "dedicated servers" who used to serve as consecrated laypersons called "diaconal ministers" through the creation of a new ordained order, "deacon."

Equipping the Saints is a powerful manifestation demonstrating that there are not two missions, one for the ordained and the other for the laity. There is only one mission: God's mission. The mission of the Crucified Christ was to God's chosen people, Israel ("the lost sheep of the house of Israel" is how Jesus put it). The mission of the risen Christ is to the world as a whole, not to the church. The mission of the church is to join Christ's mission in the world. It is this mission that defines and designs the nature of the church. It is God's mission that constitutes and commissions the church. Or in the words of theologian Jurgen Moltmann, "What we have to learn . . . is not that the church 'has' a mission, but the very reverse: the mission of Christ creates its own church. Mission does not come from the church; it is from mission and in the light of mission that the church has to be understood."[2]

LEONARD I. SWEET

E. Stanley Jones Professor of Evangelism
Drew Theological School

INTRODUCTION

Michael J. Christensen

The Priesthood of Believers Comes of Age

"The Christian religion, especially, leads straight to the abolition of the laity. The whole spirit of Jesus led his followers beyond the kind of faith in which some [persons] were priests, and he seemed to take a particular delight in showing how the ministry of the nonpriest might exceed that of the [one] to whom had been assigned a priestly function." [1]

At the advent of the third millennium of Christendom, the time has come for radical change in how to do the work of the ministry in the technological age. The transition from a modern to a postmodern worldview is nearly completed. What Lyle Schaller calls "the New Reformation of the Laity" [2] and Leonard Sweet describes as "the Postmodern

11

Reformation"[3] has already occurred. What remains of the revolution is whether the clergy or the laity will be abolished in favor of "one body with many parts."

How shall we then live in light of this new reality? How shall we minister in the Global Age of new technologies, macroeconomics, biogenetics, and quantum physics that so rapidly reorder our multiple perceptions? How shall we "equip the saints for the work of ministry" in the new era?

In 1936, Elton Trueblood asserted that "all Christians are ministers and that the mere layman is nonexistent."[4] He then went on to argue for the abolition of the laity. *Equipping the Saints* is a practical theology volume of collected narratives and case studies that assumes the "priesthood of all believers" and presents new paradigm models for *TheNextChurch.*[5] It offers new strategies to mobilize laity as ministers in a new age. It celebrates the postmodern transitions as opportunities to change—not the message but the medium of how we communicate the good news and order ourselves for ministry in the world. It calls, once and for all, for the traditional distinctions between ordained clergy and nonordained laity to be replaced with the ancient/future concept of *laos*—the called and equipped people of God. It recommends specific new forms of ministerial leadership, ecclesial structure, and ministry methods for the future church.

If every baptized Christian is called to be a minister, then we will need to consider new and innovative ways to (1) motivate for ministry, (2) actualize the "priesthood of believers," (3) organize small groups for the sake of community, (4) build leadership teams around spiritual gifts, (5) evangelize through seeker-sensitive worship, (6) learn how to "circuit ride" in the twenty-first century, and (7) reorder the ministry of the baptized. For each of these tasks a successful practitioner from various traditions has been sought out to articulate how best to implement a recommended model of ministry.

The Reverend Jessica Moffatt, who is nationally known for her expertise in mobilizing thousands of church members for "hands-on" ministry in the community, and for inspiring more than five hundred congregations to adopt her method and model, finally committed the *Motivation for Ministry* model of community outreach to written form in Chapter One. This user-friendly and highly practical model of lay mobilization, based on years of proven success, helps leaders motivate, equip, and sustain laypersons in ministries of mercy and service in their communities. The chapter includes: (1) the pastor as coach (not quarterback); (2) four ways to motivate; (3) how to offer your position, possession, passion, or preparation to God in joyful service; (4) how to identify community needs; and (5) taking church from the pew to the streets.

I asked Professor Russell Moy, my former teaching colleague at Drew Theological School who is now at Church Divinity School of the Pacific, to write Chapter Two on "The Loss and Recovery of Lay Ministry." Equipping a new generation of saints for ministry begins with solid biblical grounding and theologically informed praxis. In this chapter, Russell presents a layperson's guide to (1) the biblical, theological, and historical origins and development of *laikos* (the people of God) in church history and ministry practice; (2) how the New Testament concept of the "priesthood of believers" (1 Peter 2:9) was lost in the Patristic Period; (3) how the "priesthood of believers" was reclaimed (as doctrine) during the Protestant Reformation; and (4) what is still needed in a new Reformation of the Laity.

Chapter Three is devoted to the ministry of small groups in fostering community in a large church. Christine Anderson, a lay pastor and small group leader at Willow Creek Community Church, as well as a professional editor and writer, presents five of the most outstanding and effective models of small group ministry today: (1) Willow Creek, (2) Church of the Saviour, (3) Vineyard Christian Fellowship, (4) RENOVARÉ, and (5) Clearness Committee (Quaker). Although this is the longest chapter in the book, I decided not to edit it significantly because each case study is succinct, stellar, and the first of its kind. Choose to read first the one that attracts you the most, then go back and read them all, for each is distinct and together form a spectrum of community options in *TheNextChurch*. Brian Bauknight is now a veteran at "Team Building Through Spiritual Gifts," the subject of Chapter Four. Based on his earlier book, *Body Building: Creating a Ministry Team Through Spiritual Gifts,* Brian presents a lay ministry model organized around servant leadership and spiritual gifts for mainline churches. Denominational fears of the supernatural gifts of the Spirit and clerical reluctance to letting go of church control are faced honestly in this case study of Christ United Methodist Church of Bethel, Pennsylvania. The Reformation doctrine of the priesthood of believers is assumed and an ecclesiology of spiritual gifts, based on the presumed practice of the earliest churches, is applied in a large suburban congregation. A step-by-step congregational training plan (adapted from Willow Creek curriculum) is recommended on how to (1) determine your passion, (2) discover your spiritual gifts, (3) find your personal style of ministry, and (4) utilize your spiritual gifts for service.

Who will reach the Boomers, GenXers, and Millennial kids with the gospel? Part of the answer is multigenerational, lay-led, seeker-targeted services at larger community-oriented churches. I asked one of my exceptional doctoral students, Eric Park, associate pastor at Christ United Methodist Church, to write Chapter Five on how his popular seeker service at the church was started and what components are essential for its continued success. Willow Creek may be the instigator but is not the only model of "seeker-targeted" worship and celebration. "SUNDAY NIGHT" at Christ UMC is a mainline model of lay leadership and church growth through contemporary music, weekly drama, and thematic preaching. The chapter includes: (1) What is a "seeker"? (2) What do seekers need? (3) biblical imperatives for seeker ministry, and (4) the nonnegotiables for SUNDAY NIGHT.

Rob Duncan Jr. truly embodies the postmodern challenge to equip the saints in the technological age. Armed primarily with a laser pointer for teaching, an electronic Bible for preaching, and a laptop computer for riding the fiber-optic circuits of ministry opportunities on the World Wide Web, he is a wonder to all who work with him at Drew. No one could better write the chapter on the electronification of the church. Chapter Six, "Circuit Riding in the Twenty-First Century," of course, refers not to eighteenth- and nineteenth-century Methodist circuit riders on horseback traveling from town to town to preach, but to twenty-first-century electronic circuit riders (or perhaps Internet surfers) who create ministry opportunities on the World Wide Web. The shape of the world to come may be one giant integrated network connecting persons in innerspace to outerspace and to cyberspace. Imagine the "high-tech, high-touch" possibilities for E-vangelism, Digital Discipleship, and online pastoral care! "Wired" preachers, teachers, and evangelists will be able to "ride the circuits" in a worldwide parish and channel God's energy and grace in new and powerful ways utilizing the Net. This chapter is packed with bold ideas for the postmodern pioneer on how to navigate the new frontier, including: (1) the shift from the modern to postmodern world, (2) the new technology and how to use it, and (3) traditional functions of the pastor reconsidered in light of the above. A guided tour of Internet possibilities for ministries—including cyber-chats, bulletin boards, threaded discussions, electronic worship, online preaching, video conferencing, web page resourcing, E-letter connection, and computer prayer chains is offered in print, by means of workshops, and through online consultation by Robert Duncan Jr. @ http.//da.cihost.com/nextchurch.

As general editor, I wanted to contribute a thematic and unifying chapter for the whole. Chapter Seven, "Three Streams, One River" concludes this ambitious volume with a vision and call for the Church to reinvent itself for a new century by reclaiming the ancient metaphor of the River of God (Psalm 46) as the organizing principle for postmodern ministry. If Leonard Sweet is right about the fluidity of postmodern culture, then his vision of *AquaChurch*[6] requires a radical reordering of the ministry of the bap-

15

tized. "Three Streams, One River" refers to *worship, community,* and *mission*—three healing streams that are meant to flow as one river from the Divine source to every human heart. The chapter provides the image and substance for *TheNextChurch,* combining and incorporating the denominational distinctives and theological traditions that produced it, and responding to change and new opportunities for ministry in the global village of the twenty-first century. It is also a bridge chapter to the volume that will follow this one: *Heart of the City: The New Face of Urban Ministry.* An exhaustively researched and carefully selected bibliography on "Mobilizing Laity" by Dr. Carl Savage is included in this volume, which also includes resource recommendations by contributors. Carl's contribution is significant and helpful in that he organized the bibliography into three main categories—Premodern, Modern (General), and Postmodern resources. He then divided the General Resources for *TheNextChurch* into subcategories that support the focus of individual chapters: (1) Priesthood of All Believers, (2) Small Groups, (3) Team Building, (4) Evangelism, (5) Seeker Services, and (6) Mobilizing for Mission.

Leonard Sweet, whose own work significantly informs and shapes the Postmodern Reformation, skillfully introduces *TheNextChurch* concept in the Foreword. For Len's inspiration, mentorship, and leadership at Drew, I am truly grateful. Much of the content of this volume was presented by the chapter contributors at Drew's first National Tipple Conference—"Drew@Christ United Methodist Church, Pittsburgh"—in 1997. Other national conferences initiated by Sweet followed. These are being developed into future volumes, including: *Heart of the City: The New Face of Urban Ministry* and *Revolution in the Pulpit: Preaching and Public Theology.*

To all the contributors, and especially to my associate editor, Carl Savage, administrative assistant, Gloria Kovach, and typist Tasha Whitton, I express my indebtedness and gratitude.

Michael J. Christensen

CHAPTER ONE

Out of the Pew, into the World: Motivating for Ministry

Jessica Farish Moffatt

On the news late one night, a terrible car accident was reported. A family had been driving through Tulsa in a rain storm when the car hydroplaned and crashed into another car. Four of the five family members were killed. The only survivor was Sarah, a nine-year-old girl. The last statement of the news anchor was, "The hospital is now in search of a way to return the girl to New York to be with her other family members."

I made a mental note that the next morning I would contact our Aviation Ministry to see if they would be available to fly Sarah home. The next day, however, an early morning phone call took me into funeral preparations for a church member and I never made the call to the Aviation Ministry. I didn't remember my intentions until that night, when the news had a follow-up story about Sarah. The news anchor announced that the Aviation Ministry of First United Methodist Church would be returning Sarah home.

"That's how this is supposed to happen!" I said to the TV screen. "It is supposed to happen without me!"

The Motivation for Ministry model is designed to make just such an experience possible. It does so by helping to mobilize church members to identify needs in the community and respond to them in short-term groups according to gift, skill, interest, and training. The model was created by Dr. James Buskirk during his doctoral work at Candler School of Theology at Emory University, and was further developed by our church during my twelve-year ministry at First United Methodist Church in Tulsa (1985–1997).

It is a simple plan that works well in congregations of any size and has been used in more than five hundred churches throughout the United States. In this chapter, you will be given all the information necessary to use the Motivation for Ministry model to mobilize laity for community outreach in your own congregation.

The Way We Were

In 1985, when I accepted the position of minister of community ministries at First United Methodist Church in Tulsa, Oklahoma, I began by doing a congregational assessment. Since it was my newly created job to organize our congregation to be in hands-on ministry beyond the walls of the church, I wanted to know how many members were already involved in ministry in our community. I sent out a letter with a return postcard, asking members to indicate the ministries beyond our church in which they were involved. Out of our more than six thousand members, I received back less than thirty responses.

During the next six months, our church would move from having thirty identified peopled involved in two community ministries to having more than five hundred people involved in twenty-nine ministries. Over the next fifteen years, we would continue to have between five hundred and two thousand of our members involved in twenty-five to thirty-five hands-on ministries at any given time.

A Healthy Church Is a Church that Serves

First United Methodist Church in Tulsa is a downtown church of more than nine thousand members. The sanctuary is a Gothic cathedral. In the 1950s and 1960s our church was struggling to stay alive, when, in 1969, a Lay Witness Mission was held that started a spiritual renewal that is still going on today.

We hang all of our ministries on three tiers: Believing, Belonging, and Becoming, or to use their equivalents, *Kerygma, Koinonia,* and *Diakonia.* We believe that healthy churches have a balance of all three.

Believing / Kerygma includes preaching, teaching, praise, and worship. This happens when our minds and spirits are fed and nourished with Scripture, information, and inspiration.

Belonging / Koinonia occurs when our need for fellowship and belonging is met. It happens informally around the coffeepot, in church school classes, small groups, council meetings, and events.

Becoming / Diakonia is our servant ministry, the giving of ourselves in service to others. In our church, we talk about *diakonia* in terms of ministry *within* the walls of the church and ministry *beyond* the walls of the church. Ministry *within* the walls of the church includes ushers, church school teachers, prayer team members, care workers, those who work in the kitchen, and others who see to it that the tasks of the church are completed. It also includes financial giving, tithing, and enabling ministries with our resources.

Ministry *beyond* the walls of the church includes ministry with those in our community and the world: the poor, the rich, children, those in our neighborhoods, those at the workplace, local and foreign missions efforts. Evangelism is also included in this category.

We are convinced that for a church to be healthy, there must be a balance of all three of these areas. Motivation for Ministry is designed to help develop the area of *Diakonia,* and specifically, ministry beyond the walls of the church.

Past Motivators

Historian Daniel Boorstin is quoted as having offered this stinging observation:

> We have become a nation of observers. Many of us experience our Christian faith vicariously. We don't live the Christian life, we watch others live it. We don't experience God, we read about those who experience God. We no longer DO mission work, we SUPPORT mission work. We no longer evangelize, we hire evangelists. We no longer give our lives to the needy, we give an hour to the needy. This country has millions of people who believe in Christianity. They watch it, talk about it, televise it, sing about it, financially support it and write about it. There is just one problem. Very few are doing it![1]

How did we get in such a condition? Let me offer several possible reasons:

1. *The Request and Response Pattern* is a common leadership style found in many congregations. The pastor or organizer makes a plea for help and church members determine how they will respond. If the pastor is convincing and winsome, the response might be good. If not, the response might be poor. It depends primarily on the ability and personality of the leader.

Typically, the most common motivators used by leaders are guilt, pity, friendship, and persuasion.

Guilt: Pastors and leaders say things like, "I can't believe that with all the gifts you have, you are not in ministry!" The guilt approach uses words like "must," "should" and "ought."

Pity: This approach works on the emotions of church members. "Look at their faces. You've got to do something!"

Friendship: Many church members are willing to do what the pastor or leader is asking because of their friendship with the leader.

Persuasion: Clergy are some of the best persuaders. They are logical and passionate. They know the power of story and illustration. They know how to build good arguments.

Motivation by guilt, pity, friendship, or persuasion is often temporary because it is dependent on the energy and skills of the pastor or leader. If the pastor leaves, retires, or becomes ill, the motivation can leave as well.

2. A second motivational issue is what I call the *Clergy as Quarterback Syndrome.* This pattern is based on the false theory that only those who go to seminary and are ordained are ministers.

The church snaps the ball to the clergy and we run with it! We don't pass it. We run for the touchdown while the crowd cheers us on for our spectacular performance!

When we talk about ordination, we say the ordained are "set apart" for the ministry. Have we become so set apart that the laity do not feel a sense of their own ministry? In Korea, when Paul Yonggi Cho became seriously ill and could not continue his ministry, the leadership of the laity emerged and his congregation eventually grew into the world's largest church.[2]

The difference between a coach and a quarterback is the question, "Who is going to carry the ministry ball?" Traditionally, clergy have felt that it was their responsibility to run with the ball. The new reformation of the laity declares the reality that all God's people are ministers.

3. A third reason is the *I-Gave-at-the-Office* mind-set. With regard to those in need in our community, many church members say, "Let the agencies do it" or "Isn't that why I give to the United Way?" or "Doesn't the government have a program for those people?" or "My denomination has provisions for the needy."

4. A fourth reason is that many church members are *Sedentary Christians*. We sit in worship. We sit in Sunday school. We sit for hours surfing the Internet. We watch worship on television. We live remote-control lives. Writing a check has replaced hands-on ministry.

5. The fifth reason we may have a poor response to ministry opportunities is that we are accustomed to using the *Recruitment Pattern*. Someone is always asking my church members to do something. Every evening at about dinnertime, telephones ring as hot meals are being served. It is the school, the cancer society, or an agency asking for help or donations. Do our members place the church in this same category asking, "What does the church want from me now?"

A Better Ministry Mind-Set

Motivation for Ministry moves from "What does the church want from me?" to "How can I grow in Christ?" It is not for my pastor or my class or my church. It is out of my love for Christ, my desire to become like him and my own Christian growth.

Motivation for Ministry is ministry done on a "want to" basis and not in response to a plea or under pressure of guilt.

How do we move toward a better motivated mind-set about ministry?

1. We move from thinking in terms of *guilt, pity, friendship,* and *persuasion* to thinking in terms of *calling, gifting, invitation,* and *gratitude.*

Calling: We are each called by God into ministry through the words of Jesus Christ (Acts 1:8). Discovering our personal calling means surrendering, seeking, and listening to God about what God might have us do in the world as "witnesses" to the gospel.

Gifting: We have been given abilities, training, and resources. What gifts do we have that could be used in ministry?

22

Invitation: We are invited to follow Christ and his ethics, to live our lives following his model of love and ministry. *Gratitude:* How shall we show our thanks to God for what God has done for us? Servanthood is the core of the salvation response (John 13:14-17).

2. We preach, teach, illustrate, and reclaim the *priesthood of all believers* (1 Peter 2:9-10).

Clergy leaders become coaches, not quarterbacks. When the laypeople toss clergy the ball, we toss it back! We do our work on the sidelines. Leaders trust laypeople to run with the ministry ball and to make the touchdown.

We are currently designing a new sanctuary and we have been asking our architect, "Can we illustrate the priesthood of all believers architecturally?" In every church I have served, the preaching pulpit has been large and the lay reader's lectern very small. How can we visually illustrate the importance of the ministry of the laity?

3. We equip people for *ministry* (Ephesians 4:12).

Training, support, and encouragement go a long way in giving laypersons confidence in ministry. Equipping also includes helping persons develop a spiritual and theological foundation for doing ministry.

4. We provide a *structure* on which to hang our ministries.

People gain a way to relate their ministry to their faith, and to the life of the rest of the church. This is the function of the Motivation for Ministry model, which we are now ready to consider.

The Motivation for Ministry Model

Motivation for Ministry is a method of identifying needs in a community and responding to those needs in short-term groups of four or more according to gift, interest, skill, and training. Motivation for Ministry begins with a launch event that can take place over a two- or three-day period. The launch event includes three worship services. It can also include meetings of specific groups already in the congregation (singles, senior citizens, youth, men, women). In the peer group meetings, the specific gifts, experience, and talents for ministry of that group can be emphasized. For example, with senior citizens (we call them "keenagers"), two questions can be asked: (1) What are the blessings of being at your age and stage of life? (2) What are the difficulties? Ministry ideas can be stirred up as blessings are identified—for example, plenty of time, wisdom, sense of humor, experience, and so forth. I usually ask, "How can we turn those blessings into ministry while taking into account the limitations?" In one church, mothers of young children met to brainstorm about ministries that can be done as a family, especially those including the children.

During the first worship service, the theology of lay ministry is communicated, the priesthood of all believers is affirmed, and the characteristics of a healthy church are described. The Motivation for Ministry model is explained and the congregation is asked if they want to be a part of such an endeavor. Before the service is concluded, participants are asked to take the next twenty-four hours to consider what the community needs might be. They are urged to read the newspaper, listen to the news, ask agencies, call their mayor or city councillor, be aware of needs at their health club, neighborhood, and workplace. The congregation is told that at the next worship service, those needs will be collected and compiled.

The focus of the second worship service is on celebration of laypersons in ministry throughout our nation. Stories of creative lay involvement in mission can be told to "prime the pump" for idea collecting. At the end of the service, a card with one question is provided for each person: What needs do you see in our community to which you wish our church was in ministry? Persons are instructed to be specific in suggesting community needs. For example, rather than write, "We need to show love to kids in our city," someone might suggest an after-school ministry partnering retired persons with elementary-school students. It is important to emphasize that the cards are not to be signed and that persons are not committing to any ministry by offering a suggestion.

After this second worship service, the cards are compiled by similarity of suggestions and listed with room numbers beside each category. In our second worship service in 1985, we received sixteen hundred suggestions of ministry needs in Tulsa. That night, on my living-room floor, I began to make stacks of similar suggestions. By the time I had finished, there were forty-nine different types of ministry suggested in those sixteen hundred cards. When I listed the name of the ministry, I described the idea using the actual language from the cards.

At the beginning of the worship service on the third night, lists of potential ministries with room numbers are distributed as people gather. There is always an excitement as people read the list. The focus of the third worship service is on the layperson identifying his or her gifts, skills, and interests. The following question might be presented in this service: "What position, possession, passion, or preparation do you have that could be used in ministry?" A "position" might be a job, a relational connection, or a special resource. A "possession" could be a lawn mower, a swimming pool, a bicycle, an airplane. "Passion" is what a person loves to do—work with children, work in the garden, play golf. Ask people to think about how a passion could become a ministry.

"Preparation" includes education, training, and skill. I ask, "Has God provided a particular education for you that can now be used in ministry? Have you been to law school or medical school or have other training? Have you been to the police academy or taught school? How could you use your training in ministry?"

After our worship service the final night, the congregation is instructed, "Go to the room of the ministry that interests you the most." There are a few rules about those ministry groups:

1. There needs to be four or more persons in the room in order to proceed. If there are fewer than four, participants are invited to go to their second choice.
2. Ministry is done on a six-month basis. At the end of six months, persons are invited to stay in the same ministry group, change ministries, create a new ministry group, or take a break from this form of ministry altogether.
3. A group can "die" at any time without guilt. We promised not to say, "Oh, but that was such a good ministry! I can't believe you are quitting!" Motivation for Ministry allows people to rest when they need to and to come back into a ministry when they are ready. This helps prevent burnout.

We told them that when they got to their rooms, they were to take twenty minutes and answer the following four questions that would be on a page in the room:

1. What, in general, do we want to accomplish?
2. Who are the resource persons to help us accomplish it?
3. Who will contact those resource people for our next meeting?
4. When and where will we meet again?

Groups were given a recorder's sheet to return to a box at the altar at the end of the evening with the name of the new group and the next time and place of meeting. This information can be published in the next newsletter and bulletin so that those unable to participate in the Motivation for Ministry launch event can attend the second meeting of a group.

On the third night of our first Motivation for Ministry event, thirty-nine new ministry groups were formed, each having four or more persons in them. Some groups had as many as sixty, others barely had four. Six weeks later, after a natural attrition, we had twenty-nine strong, new ministries.

The following list gives an idea of some of the ministries that started that night:

Medical Clinic:	Provides free medical care. Called "The Great Physician," this mobile medical clinic is housed in the back of a station wagon that travels with teams to the government housing complexes one night each week. Doctors and nurses see the patients while nonmedical volunteers watch the children, befriend those waiting, and pray with those who would like prayer.
Wheelchair Ministry:	Provides wheelchairs, walkers, crutches, and other equipment to those who need them.
Pedalers for Christ:	Distributes new or refurbished bicycles to children who need encouragement.
"Eye Care" Eye Clinic:	Provides eye exams, glasses, and contacts for those who cannot afford them.
Legal Counseling Ministry:	Offers legal services and counseling for persons in need of assistance.
Aviation Ministry:	Provides transportation by way of private airplane for out-of-state medical care, funeral transportation, missions deliveries, and such.
Dental Clinic Ministry:	Provides dental care for those experiencing dental pain. This ministry specializes in root canals.
Destination Discovery:	Serves the children of the government housing complexes with after-school tutoring, seasonal gifts, and special events.
Used Car Ministry:	Acquires used or broken down cars, repairs them, and donates them to families in need.
Ministry with the Hearing Impaired:	Provides interpretation of Sunday worship services and offers fellow-

ship opportunities and other services for the hearing impaired.

Card Ministry: Creates and delivers personalized greeting cards to persons who are homebound or in need of encouragement.

Transportation Ministry: Drives persons to doctors' appointments, church, grocery store, and such.

First Fruits Food Ministry: Provides fresh food at a low cost for those who wish to participate in a food cooperative.

Life Light Ministry with Unwed Mothers: Provides support, maternity clothes, baby items, and friendship for unmarried mothers.

Ministry with the Poor, Hungry, and Homeless: Works with our local United Methodist agency and other groups to provide food, clothing, shelter, and encouragement for families and individuals.

Jobs First Ministry with the Unemployed: Provides job placement services matching the skills of unemployed persons with known job opportunities and assists in résumé preparation.

Christian Business Ministry: Gives support and training for businesspersons who want to establish their businesses on Christian principles.

Prison Ministry: Cares for those who are incarcerated through visits, Bible studies, worship services, and other events; cares for the families of prisoners.

Moving in the Spirit: Moves the furniture and household goods of those in need.

Adult Tutoring Ministry: Teaches illiterate adults to read and write through a local literacy center.

Christian Financial Ministry: Provides seminars, classes, and resources to teach biblical principles of

	managing money; offers financial counseling.
Odd Jobs Ministry:	Completes household tasks for those unable to do so for themselves.
Tax Preparation Ministry:	Assists persons in the preparation of individual income tax returns.
Adopt-a-Cop:	Supports in prayer police officers who would like to have a prayer partner.
Flower Ministry:	Delivers individual arrangements of the flowers used in Sunday worship to those who are homebound or hospitalized.
Habitat for Humanity:	Builds homes through our local Habitat for Humanity organization.
Friendship Partners with International Students:	Initiates family-like friendships with foreign students for the school year.

If I, as the minister of community ministries, had tried to think of ministries for our congregation, I would never have thought of many of them! I *know* I would not have thought of a used car ministry or an aviation ministry! (Note that a few of the ministries work with  local agencies under agency training and supervision.)

While we will never do the launch event again, every six months we hold a new Motivation for Ministry event, asking for suggestions of needs, and matching gifts and interests with those needs. In the fall, we use the Sunday morning worship services to hear from those who have been in ministry. In the spring, we invite a guest speaker to inspire us. We have had Tony Campolo, Bishop Leontine Kelly, Norman Neaves, Evelyn Laycock, and Bishop Dan Solomon speak at our spring emphasis.

Model Distinctives

Every suggestion is taken seriously. Some of the suggestions have been very unusual! But we communicate that every idea is valid.

There must be an atmosphere of "no guilt." This was one of the most difficult leadership shifts to make. Guilt is so effective! Extending the invitation to cease a ministry puts people in the posture of explaining why they want to stay in a ministry. Ministry is genuinely done out of "want to." I contact each ministry group every six months and encourage them to quit. What a nice turn of the tables it is to listen to the explanations of why people want to continue in ministry!

Each group determines its own course. Each ministry group determines how they will be organized and how they will be trained for the tasks to which they feel called. For most ministries, on-the-job training works best. Some ministries will require specialized training, which they will arrange for themselves. The fewer meetings before the actual ministry begins, the better. Once the basic perimeters of the ministry are established and any training begun, groups should get on with the ministry as quickly as possible.

It is important to identify real needs. There are two common reasons ministry groups die. Either the group was not focused on a real need, or the group was not successful in finding the ministry recipients.

The first step in identifying real needs is to get to know your community. Contact the social service agencies. Call other churches in your area to see what they have discovered and what they are doing. Contact the police department and the schools. What is the unemployment rate of your city? Why? Stay in touch with your city hot line. Who is calling? What do they need? Ask those in need what they need. United Methodist Bishop Dan Solomon suggests going door to door in opportune neighborhoods, explaining at each home, "I am from First United Methodist Church and we are wondering what we might do to be of help to you."

Once you have all this information, bring your community in to your sanctuary, into your sermons, into your liturgy and your newsletters.

Create a Ministry Network. Not long after launching our first ministry groups, we realized that the groups needed a way to connect to one another for encouragement, resourcing, and accountability. So we created a Community Ministries Network. This group has a representative from each ministry group and a representative from each of our twenty-six adult church school classes.

Once a month, on a Monday night, we gather at 5:30 P.M. for a light supper. After dinner, we go around the circle for comments from each person. Each ministry group representative tells what the group is doing and describes ways in which church school classes might be involved. Each church school class representative talks about individual class ministry projects and informs ministry groups of those in their classes interested in ministry projects. The following Sunday, class representatives give a Community Ministries report filled with information and inspiration.

The meeting of the Community Ministries Network is an excellent way for the coordinator of the ministries to stay in touch with, provide resources to, and watch for problem areas in the ministry groups. For example, early on, we realized we needed a no-fund-raising policy. The Community Ministries Network, not the coordinator, developed the policy.

New ministries can be started at any time. If there are new ministry ideas between Motivation for Ministry events, a meeting time and place can be announced. If there are four or more people, the new ministry can begin and be incorporated into the "ministry menu."

Is it necessary to have a staff person facilitate the Motivation for Ministry model? No. The model works beautifully when a volunteer lay leader facilitates the model. Some churches work through the nominations committee to determine a potential coordinator. Others work through the missions or outreach committee.

How does it work in the smaller church? Smaller churches will usually launch between three and nine new ministries at the first launch event. The groups can be coordinated by a lay coordinator who connects them to the governing church body.

Motivational Strategies

Gain an Identity as a Church

Two years after beginning the Motivation for Ministry model, we decided to change our church motto to reflect our new ministry emphasis. Our motto used to be, "First United Methodist Church, a friendly church, where people care and Jesus Christ is Lord." The addition of two words helped us embrace our new identity as a servant church. Now, our motto is "First United Methodist Church, a friendly church, where people care *and serve* and Jesus Christ is Lord." We began to refer to our church as a servant church while we journeyed to become one.[3]

Preach to Deploy

The use of illustration in preaching is the best way to stir up a congregation for hands-on ministry. We need excellent theology, but we also need to ignite the imaginations of our church members with stories of creativity and passion. I am continually collecting stories of laypersons in ministry. When we began to use the model, we had to tell stories of laypersons in other churches, but as we progressed, we could use the innovative ideas of our own members to illustrate the creative power of God in us.

Preaching and worship themes we have used include:

By their fruits ye shall know them. Matthew 6:16
Let us be doers of the word and not hearers only. James 1:22

Who is the Lazarus at our doorstep? Luke 16:19-31
Separating sheep from goats. Matthew 25:32
Who is my neighbor? Luke 10:35-37
Go the second mile. Matthew 5:41
As you sow also shall you reap. 2 Corinthians 9:6

One-on-One Nurture

Church members regularly come to my office, inspired by
the idea of hands-on ministry in the community, but in need
of direction and focus.

A woman named Kathryn came to my office.

"I would like to be in ministry," she said, "but I can't think
of anything I could do."

"Tell me about yourself," I said to her. "Tell me about your
family. How many children do you have?"

"Eight."

"Eight! And you say you can't think of any skills you may
have? How do you feed a family of ten economically?" I
asked.

"I suppose I do know how to feed a big family on a small
monthly budget," she said. "I save hundreds of dollars every
month with coupons. I know all the tricks! Could that be a
ministry?"

Within weeks, Kathryn and three other women had
organized a ministry at the government housing complex
called "Mom to Mom." It is a ministry of teaching mothers
how to serve economical meals, how to devise a household budget, and how to bring order into the daily family
regimen.

Provide Short-Term, Hands-on Ministry Experience

A one-day or weekend ministry project is sometimes the
best way to introduce people to community ministry. We
have found that offering an afternoon to work with a Habitat
for Humanity project or a one-day Volunteer-in-Mission

effort gives church members a glimpse of what it's like to be in hands-on ministry. Soon, they are ready to think about being a part of a ministry group.

Give Opportunity for Testimony

In addition to the fall emphasis where church members describe in worship their ministry experiences, we look for other ways church members might speak of the joy of being in ministry. Council meetings, board meetings, "ministry moments" in worship throughout the year, and newsletter articles are excellent opportunities to invite those in ministry to tell their stories. With exposure, servanthood can be contagious!

Be Consistent

It was important in our congregation that if we announced we would have a Motivation for Ministry event every six months, we actually have one every six months! Our second Motivation for Ministry event at the first six-month marker was not as strong as our first, but our third one was stronger than the second and our fourth was stronger than any of the others. It took several six-month periods for our church members to take seriously this was our method.

Use a Variety of Media to Inform and Inspire

One year, we used banners depicting each ministry. Every ministry created a banner at an evening banner workshop. On Motivation for Ministry Sunday, thirty-two community ministry group representatives marched into the sanctuary during the opening hymn with banners. It was a beautiful sight and an excellent way to celebrate what God was doing in our congregation.

Other years, we have videotaped those in ministry and shown the video in worship or church school. We have placed stickers on people's lapels at the door of the sanctuary and have effectively used a trail of footprints from the pews to the asphalt on the street (our *Out of the Pew, Into the Streets!* campaign). One year, we wrote a drama from Matthew 25 where persons were "planted" in the audience and spoke out conversationally to the liturgist as he read each line of scripture: "Lord, when did we see you hungry? . . . "

Do Not Forget the Youth

For every Motivation for Ministry event, we create a strategy to intentionally include the youth of our congregation. It is important to take time in the youth group meetings to explain the model, to present the theology of the "priesthood of all believers" and to encourage the youth to find a ministry group. We brainstorm with the group about ministry needs in the community so they will be prepared to make suggestions on the idea cards. We bring in a city councillor or an agency director as a special speaker. We use illustrations of creative kids in ministry.

One year, we used the Motivation for Ministry model with the youth department apart from the rest of the congregation. In the youth room, kids wrote ministry ideas on youth-only cards. They took a dinner break while the cards were categorized and room numbers assigned to each topic. After dinner, they went to the room of the topic that interested them the most. Youth convened the groups and adult sponsors gave support as needed. The first year we did this, we had seven new youth ministry groups, ranging from serving meals at our local homeless shelter to painting a house through an agency that serves the homebound.

The Next Step

After many years of doing ministry on a short-term basis, it became clear to us that some ministries needed long-term attention. Ministries with children who had experienced abandonment, for example, needed adults who would partner with children for longer than a six-month period. We also had an opportunity to purchase and renovate a HUD house and sponsored a family who lived there, which required extended commitment. In addition, we learned of systemic changes needed in our community that could be influenced only with long-term ministry.

To meet these long-term needs, we launched a second phase of ministry called Urban Outreach, where we organize long-term groups to meet systemic needs. We offer sign-up opportunities for these ministries at the same time we have the Motivation for Ministry event every six months. As we invite people to participate in these extended ministries, we are careful not to use recruitment language or to motivate by guilt, pity, friendship, and persuasion. We continue to emphasize calling, passion, gifting, and interest.

Applying the Model to Other Ministry Areas

Several years ago, we were ready to start new prayer ministries in our congregation. We had invited a special speaker to spend a weekend at our church inspiring us toward new prayer initiatives. Given our community ministries experience, we knew that ministries were healthiest when they were created by laypersons in response to genuine needs. We had an idea. What if we used the Motivation for Ministry model to launch new prayer ministries?

We designed the prayer emphasis weekend so that during the second session, we would collect ideas for new prayer ministries. We handed out a card that said, "What prayer needs do you see in our church and community?" We compiled the suggestions, placed room numbers beside each category, and after our final session with our guest speaker we invited people to attend the prayer ministry that interested them the most. We instructed them that if there were not four or more in the room, they should make a second choice.

We began more than a dozen new prayer initiatives that night, including prayer walking, drive-by praying, prayer in the sanctuary during worship services, a prayer room, prayer for schools and students, prayer for the ministerial staff at staff meetings, Abraham's blessing, and more.

The timing of the new prayer initiatives was remarkable. Our church had experienced a very difficult year. Two events had worn us to an emotional frazzle.

On a Friday afternoon at 5:00 P.M., I paged one of our maintenance workers and asked him to help me put some heavy boxes in my car. He was prompt, polite, and professional. None of us knew that he was a drug user. After helping me, he took a smoke break, at which time he smoked a great deal of crack cocaine. By 5:40 P.M., he had strangled and killed our secretary. He then stole a car and fled the state.

We were stunned. We were crushed. Our staff wept for weeks. We had only begun to work on our grieving when the Murrah Federal Building in Oklahoma City was bombed, putting pain upon pain. We were emotionally broken. Our ministers needed ministry.

Our prayer emphasis weekend, which had been planned for months, came just weeks after these two horrendous crimes. When we asked our church members, "What prayer needs do you see?" they said to the ministers, "*You*. We see the leaders of our congregation in need of prayer and healing."

Two different staff prayer ministries were launched during our prayer emphasis weekend. One of them was a group from our men's ministry who asked if they could come into our staff meeting and pray for us before we began. Every Tuesday, they circled our conference table and stood behind our chairs. They put their strong hands on our shoulders and prayed for us.

There is one Tuesday afternoon etched in my mind that I will never forget. It was about eight weeks after the bombing in Oklahoma City. The men encircled our table and announced, "We'd like to do something a little different today. First, we would like for you to raise your hands. Raise them high. Each of you should raise both of them." Then they began to talk about a variety of things. Our arms grew tired, then heavy, then they hurt. "Oh, are you getting tired?" one of the men asked.

"Yes!" we exclaimed.

"Good," he said. "Keep your hands up while I read to you from Exodus 17:11-12:

> So it came about when Moses held his hand up, that Israel prevailed, and when he let his hand down, Amalek prevailed. But Moses' hands were heavy. Then they took a stone and put it under him, and he sat on it; and Aaron and Hur supported his hands, one on one side and one on the other. Thus his hands were steady until the sun set. (NASB)

The men then put their hands under our arms and held up our weary limbs. And while we received sweet relief from their support, they prayed for our strength, healing, and renewal. With that act, our clergy lost all sense of boundaries between who is and who is not a minister.

For ten years, I had trained my congregation to respond to the hurting, the poor, and those in need. Never did I dream that I would be the one who was hurting and that the need would be my own. Today, I minister in concert with other ministers (clergy and lay) knowing that together we can best accomplish the work of the ministry.

CHAPTER TWO

The Loss and Recovery of Lay Ministry

Russell Moy

"The great ideal of the abolition of the laity has caught hold of [people] fitfully, but it has never been seriously followed in the Church at large, at least not since the first Christian century." [1]

It may seem ironic that an ordained minister is writing this chapter on lay ministry. However, as a seminary professor, I have observed how churches often do not utilize the skills and gifts of the laity. The result is overworked pastors with churches full of passive pewsitters. Despite impassioned pleas from the pulpit, there are endless needs for ministerial volunteers in the life and mission of the church. Pastors are tempted (as I have been) to randomly recruit committee members and hope they have the abilities for the position. Pastors, becoming desperate, are like cowboys "lassoing" the slow (and unlucky) horses to be Sunday school teachers! This approach "puts the cart before the horse" by putting church positions first and then trying to find people to fit into them.

Empowering laity for ministry is more than just matching people to the needs of the institutional  church. Ministry expands beyond the four walls of the church to include the workplace and family life. A connection must be made between Sunday worship and the rest of the week. Because of their spiritual giftedness through baptism, laypeople are ministers and priests called to serve God through their jobs, family, and relationships. For this role they need "equipping"—leadership development by clergy and lay mentors.

A vision of lay ministry will be presented in this chapter based upon the New Testament ideal of the church as God's own people and priests (1 Peter 2:9) who are called according to divine purpose (Romans 8:28) and gifted for ministry (Ephesians 4:12). However, the gradual development of the clergy over and against the laity can be traced back to the Patristic Age. The dominance of the "clergy paradigm" eroded the ministry of laity and the prevalence of "priesthood of believers" was lost for over a millennium. Briefly recovered by Martin Luther during the Protestant Reformation, the "priesthood of all believers" was lost again as a new clergy paradigm of preaching was developed. This relegated laypeople to passive "hearers" of sermons instead of active "doers" of shared ministry. A New Reformation of the Laity is now needed at the dawn of the third millennium.

Let us briefly examine (1) the New Testament vision of lay ministry, (2) how the model was lost by the church fathers in the second century, (3) how the priesthood of believers was restored (at least in doctrine) in the Protestant Reformation; and finally, (4) the New Reformation of the Laity.

The New Testament Model

Ephesians 4:12: "To Equip the Saints for the Work of Ministry"

Paul's letter to the church at Ephesus describes the variety of spiritual gifts that Christ gives to his church apostles, prophets, evangelists, and pastor-teachers (4:11). The purpose of these gifts is to "equip the saints for the work of ministry" (4:12). However, in the King James Version, it is translated "for the perfecting of the saints, for the work of ministry." What is the difference? It is the "fatal comma" between the phrase "for the perfecting of the saints" and "for the work of ministry." With this erroneous comma, the King James Version implies that there are two purposes for these spiritual gifts; the perfecting of the saints and also the work of ministry.

By separating these phrases with punctuation (absent in the Greek), the King James Version denies laypeople their ministry. Why? Because the purpose of apostles, prophets, evangelists, and pastor-teachers is not for the "perfection of the saints," but to completely equip Christians to do "the work of ministry."

Thus Paul's criterion for successful ministry is utilizing your people's spiritual gifts for varied ministry. He does not mention the size of your congregation or your church budget. Rather it is training laypeople to do ministry inside and outside the church walls.

1 Peter 2:9: "You [All] Are . . . God's Own People"

The Greek word for "people" is *laos* from which we get the world *laity.* The term *clergy* comes from the Greek word *kleros,* which does not mean priesthood. Rather it means inheritance and being chosen by lot.

41

So, ironically, in the church described in the New Testament, *everyone is a clergyperson* (in the biblical sense of that term) *and no one is a layperson* (in the usual sense of that term).[2]

From our use of the word *laity,* it would seem that the Greek word *laos* would often appear in the writings of the early church fathers. But it does not. In fact, *laos* was used most often to refer to common things not set apart for religious purposes.

One of the earliest church fathers was Clement of Rome, a second generation Christian who lived just after the apostles. He used *laos* in a distinctive way to refer to a clan of people. In his letter to the Corinthians, written about 95 C.E., Clement contrasted the priests and Levites with the *laos.* He also used *laos* as an adjective when he referred to the "layman's code."

> The high priest is given his particular duties: the priests are assigned their special place, while on the Levites particular tasks are imposed. The layman is bound by the layman's code. (40:5)[3]

Clement used the Old Testament as a pattern for Christian worship. Or perhaps he used a Roman hierarchy that he justified in Old Testament terms. In this priestly hierarchy, specific responsibilities were given to respective orders: the high priest, priests, Levites, and laity. The *laos* were listed last as they were "bound by the layman's code." Although Clement does not specify what was "the layman's code," he "insisted on the liturgical competence of the layman, however limited it might be."[4] Yet already lay persons had to submit to a "code" set by the "priests."

The term *laos* did not appear again in the writings of the church fathers until early in the third century. It was not until the time of Clement of Alexandria when the concept of the laity (as distinct from clergy) emerged. "It is possible, then, to say that Christianity existed for about two hundred years without a laity."[5] The gradual development of the order of clergy was inevitable as the church gained imperial patronage and clerical privileges that began with the conversion of the Roman emperor Constantine in 313 C.E.

1 Peter 2:9: "You [All] Are . . . a Royal Priesthood"

Not only are we God's own people, we also are God's royal priesthood. As indicated in this one verse, every Christian is both "priest" and "people" so we can truly be called a "clerical people."[6] In this letter to Christian exiles and resident aliens in Asia Minor, Peter transfers the title of "priest" to the whole people of God. Instead of a group of Levites and priests chosen by their heredity, every Christian shares the corporate dimension of the priesthood. To indicate the plural "you" in the Greek, I have translated it as "you all." In our individualistic culture, this verse can be easily misunderstood to mean that each Christian is a priest. Rather, the church is a kingdom of priests elected by God to be sanctified and to offer up spiritual sacrifices of worship, prayer, and service.

This corporate sense of priesthood was affirmed by the second-century apologist, Justin Martyr, who wrote:

> being inflamed by the word of his [Christ's]) calling, we are the true high-priestly race of God. . . . Now God receives sacrifices from no one, except through His priests.[7]

Also, the "contemporary Athenian apologist Aristides asserted that all Christians could trace their genealogy from the High Priest Jesus Christ."[8]

In the writings of the early church fathers "the doctrine of the universal priesthood has a central place," according to Cyril Eastwood. It is directly linked with the Eucharist, the unity of the church, church discipline, and the church's missionary task. "The Church as a High Priestly Race, and . . . the offering of spiritual sacrifices . . . are mentioned in the writings of all the Fathers."[9]

How the Model Was Lost

In addition to this corporate priesthood, the church from its birth recognized leaders such as the apostles and prophets, defined by their spiritual gifts. One of the church's tasks was to develop and clarify leadership roles in the congregation as various people became leaders when different spiritual gifts were needed. The disadvantage of informal leadership was that these charismatic teachers could have different and even contrary messages as they competed for positions of authority.

By the end of the New Testament era when the original leaders died out, there was the question of succession and the need for "some recognized appointment procedure, especially when the possible candidates were not so unmistakeably endowed with *charismata* as the previous leaders had been."[10] Charisma was thus formalized into church offices, which then replaced charismatic spiritual gifts.

> Already, by the end of the New Testament era, the authors of the Pastoral Epistles, the *First Letter of Clement*, and the *Didache* were insisting on a more stable, predictable, and unifying kind of leadership. They called for regularly appointed officers, given titles such as "elder/presbyter," "overseer/bishop," and "servant-deacon."[11]

Private revelatory claims of prophets and teachers were questioned when they were contrary to prevailing beliefs. This difficulty of discerning true prophets from false ones resulted in the bishop taking over their teaching functions. Prophets and teachers who did not submit to this episcopal authority found refuge for their independent ministries in Montanism, Marcionism, and other movements judged as heretical by the mainstream church.

Ignatius of Antioch, around 117 C.E., insisted that "the bishop preside at the assembly for worship."[12] This view of a bishop's official sacramental role became widespread by the end of the second century. When the bishop could not attend, presbyters were designated to take his place. During this period, local bishops and presbyters were called "priests." Deacons, who also helped lead the worship service, were called "Levites" in association with the Israelite priestly tribe.

Liturgical functions in the church became clericalized as early as the third century in the Apostolic tradition of Hippolytus where formal prayers were used to ordain a bishop, a presbyter, and a deacon. Each was to "pray for the gifts of the Spirit which are thought to be requisite for each office."[13]

> The idea of a ministerial priesthood was not in competition with that of the universal priesthood of all Christians. Even for Irenaeus, who thought of the church's presbyters as "masters" possessing the charism of truth, all the disciples of Christ were priests and no special subject could, in his opinion, make an exclusive claim to have the right to make an offering.[14]

However, a paradigm shift took place in the fourth century when the concept of priesthood was reconstructed. The individual authority of a priest was enlarged so that the "High Priestly Race gave place to a High Priestly Class, and the spiritual sacrifices gave place to a priestly sacrifice offered to God in the Eucharist."[15] One result was that "from the third century onward, the need for the people of God to be split into two groups—clergy and faithful believers—was postulated in all ecclesiological teaching."[16]

The Rediscovery of the Priesthood of All Believers

This priestly hierarchy continued for over a millennium until "the priesthood of all believers" was rediscovered by Martin Luther. This was his rallying cry against the Roman Catholic Church, which sparked the Protestant Reformation in the sixteenth century. For Luther, each Christian was a

45

priest because of his or her baptism and faith. No mediator was needed because, as a priest, each Christian "has an office of sacrifice, not the Mass, but the dedication of himself to the praise and obedience of God, and to bearing the Cross."[17]

Luther clearly states that through baptism, we become priests: "The fact is that our baptism consecrates us all without exception, and makes us all priests."[18] If all believers are priests, then they have the right to preach the gospel, even though all may not exercise this right. Yet this right to preach, says Luther, must be confirmed and authorized by the congregation.

The same is true in the administration of the sacraments. For Luther,

> all have the same authority in regard to the Word and the Sacraments, although no one has the right the administer them without the consent of the members of his Church, and the call of the majority. . . . The priesthood is simply the ministry of the Word.[19]

While all have the authority to be priests to administer the Word and sacrament, not all are called by God to exercise this right. Thus the priesthood of all believers did not abolish the ordained ministry for Luther. A ministerial order was needed despite the dangers of an ordained hierarchy. Ministers were called by God to serve a congregation of "priests" whose life was a sacrifice of prayer, worship, and service. Therefore the context of their ordained ministry was the universal priesthood that belonged to all Christians by virtue of their baptism. Thus, while recognizing the priesthood of all believers, Luther maintained an order of clergy that would preach and celebrate the sacraments.

John Calvin also held the view that ordained clergy and baptized believers were priests. He believed there are two levels of calling: a general call to ministry for everyone, and a "secret" call to those called out to preach.

While Luther and Calvin believed in the priesthood of all believers, their emphasis on preaching the Word resulted in another clerical priviledge where ministry is narrowly equated with the clergy. When laypeople became passive hearers of preaching and presiding, the Reformation rallying cry of the "priesthood of all believers" was soon lost. According to William Countryman, "Most Protestants who rejected the medieval priesthood at the Reformation put comparable forms of ordained ministry in its place."[20]

Developing over the centuries, the clergy paradigm viewed ministers as a channel through which laypeople received grace. In this priestly hierarchy, the clergy were the "real" Christians who were serious about understanding and living out their faith, and the laity were their followers. The clerical paradigm assumed the spiritual and moral superiority of ordained ministers over the lay believers, reducing them to the role of second-class citizens. A more modern view sees laypeople as "clients" of a professionalized clergy who services them with their specialized knowledge. In these excessive implications of the clerical paradigm, lay and clergy are placed in opposition to each other. Thus the domination of the clergy over laity has continued to be the pattern for much of the church's history.

A New Reformation of the Laity

From this brief survey of church history focused on laity, it is apparent that the New Testament concepts of distributed spiritual gifts and the priesthood of believers were lost as they became concentrated in the person of the bishop and other clerical officials in the hierarchical church structure.

Yet eliminating the clergy is not the answer. If this is done, then a new kind of clergy will replace it. When the Temple was destroyed in 70 C.E., Judaism developed a rabbinical "priesthood" to replace the priests and Levites of Temple worship. Only the Quakers have successfully resisted this class pattern of sacramental priests and ministers.

But if it is not a question of abolishing the clergy, perhaps abolishing the laity can renew our understanding of the priestly ministry of the baptized. After all, ordination is not a separate calling; rather it is a recognition of one's gifts and calling by fellow priests to be a leader in the congregation.

> The ordained person is thus primarily a sign, a sacrament of the priesthood of all Christians, which is the priesthood of Christ. . . . The universal reality is that the ordained person becomes a sacrament of the fundamental priestly ministry shared by all with Christ.[21]

Empowering laypeople as priests or ministers can be threatening to professional pastors who do not want to see their clerical authority and privileges diminished. Can sharing ministry with laypeople reduce pastoral status and prestige? What should be the relationship between clergy and lay? Answers to these questions will be based on the interconnectedness of clergy and laypeople. Clergy are not to be defined over against the laity, rather each ordering of gifts and calling needs redefinition so their interrelatedness can be more harmonious. To overcome the clergy-lay dichotomy, ordination must be viewed as a recognition for a ministry by laypeople who are also ministers in their own right. The noted church consultant, Lyle Schaller, predicts that lay ministry will become the norm for ministry in the twenty-first century. Already, there is a major transformation of church structures:

> The role of the clergy and program staff will shift from conducting and micromanaging ministry to "challenging, enlisting, training, placing, nurturing, and supporting volunteers who do the ministry."[22]

In this way, the church of the new millennium can again reclaim the New Testament model of spiritual gifts and royal priesthood in empowering laity for ministry.

CHAPTER THREE

Life Together: Reclaiming the Ministry of Small Groups

Christine M. Anderson

"How very good and pleasant it is when kindred live together in unity!"

(Psalm 133:1)

Perfect community is to be found at the intersection of the two segments of the cross, where those who are reconciled with God are reconciled together—where we love God with all we have and we love our neighbor as ourselves. . . . It is the place of transformation.[1]

One of the most chilling illustrations of hell I've heard describes it not in terms of fire, brimstone, and gnashing teeth, but as the "utter loss of community." With the understanding that "God's dream for the human race is community," heaven provides the ultimate expression of oneness with God and one another. Hell, in contrast, is a place where God, hence community, is not to be found. As my pastor, John Ortberg, states: "All the things that make community possible—humility, servanthood, courtesy, love, honesty—these are all gifts of God . . . hell is the mirror opposite."[2]

To the degree that our lifestyles and culture mitigate against deep and meaningful relationships in our families, social circles, and houses of worship, it is not difficult to find evidence of a kind of hell-on-earth today. As society has become increasingly fragmented, we have moved from a culture rooted in community connectedness to what Cornel West calls a "hotel society." In such a society, one may live in the company of others, but the connections are tenaciously superficial and unrelentingly transitory. Addressing the loss of communal culture at the close of the twentieth century, Mary Pipher writes, "People stopped knowing one another in a variety of roles across time and place. We don't live near our cousins or grow old with the same people we were born with. As we approach the end of our century, we all live among strangers."[3] If this is indeed the case, and if people of faith are called to live out God's dream of community (what Dietrich Bonhoeffer describes as "life together"[4]), how can the church support and facilitate this corporate reality?

Though the prognosis appears grim, it is far from hopeless. In recent years, many churches and Christian organizations have made great strides in reclaiming community as a fundamental value. The principle means of recovery is not a radically new idea, but a revolutionary old one. Drawing on the legacy and pioneering ministry of John Wesley, the reclamation of community is being accomplished through innovative adaptations of the centuries-old practice we now call "small groups." In their day, Wesley's Methodist societies, band meetings, and class meetings,[5] provided an effective means of community and pastoral care because they met people where they were and offered a meaningful framework for spiritual growth. Though members of Roman

Catholic monastic orders had known the value of communal nurture and oversight for centuries, it was a revolutionary concept for the laity in Wesley's time. In committing themselves to an intimate faith community rooted in mutual care and accountability, Methodist society, band, and class members had access to a kind of spiritual strength and stamina that equal solitary effort could never sustain. This was, in fact, Wesley's pastoral genius—the creation of a practical means for discipleship and the care of souls in which people of faith were empowered and equipped to care for one another. In its simplest formulation, it is the spiritual equivalent of "all for one, and one for all."

In the following pages you will read about five unique models for doing life together. These include case studies of Willow Creek Community Church in South Barrington, Illinois; Church of the Saviour in Washington, D.C.; Vineyard Christian Fellowship in Anaheim, California; RENOVARÉ, a spiritual formation movement based in Englewood, Colorado; and the Quaker discernment practice known as a "clearness committee." Though hardly an exhaustive representation, each small-group model has proven extraordinarily effective in accomplishing its goals. To put a human face on the description of the models, each begins with the real story of a person whose life has been impacted by participation in that kind of group. The small group models themselves are articulated in large part not by theorists, but by practitioners whose work is devoted to small-group ministry. Considering that John Wesley has been called the father of today's small-group concept,[6] I believe he would find much to commend in the models that follow.

We begin with Willow Creek Community Church, a church whose pioneering "seeker-targeted" approach and remarkable growth have garnered considerable coverage in national media such as *Time, Newsweek, The New York Times* and ABC network news, just to name a few. In the early nineties, Willow Creek charted a course for its ministry that has now positioned it to become a pioneering leader in community-building small groups. Though the church is large (currently it has over sixteen thousand in weekend attendance), its approach to small groups can be and is being successfully implemented by churches of less than one hundred members. I am most familiar with this model because Willow Creek is my church home and the place where I am a small-group leader.

Willow Creek Community Church
South Barrington, Illinois

A church with small groups is a church that basically looks at small groups as a program. . . . A church of small groups says that the way we will do life and ministry at this church is through small groups, in every area and every department. That's our approach.

—Bill Donahue,
Executive Director of Small Group Ministries,
Willow Creek Association[7]

Jarrett Pautz, Member of a Seeker Small Group

Jarrett Pautz, a twenty-eight-year-old operations manager for a manufacturing firm, began attending Willow Creek Community Church about a year ago when friends invited him and his fiancée, Marlo, to a seeker-targeted weekend service. Although he was raised Roman Catholic, Jarrett grew dissatisfied with his childhood faith during his college years, a time he describes as one of "losing sight of things."[8] Commenting on what made him receptive to the invitation to Willow Creek, Jarrett reflects, "When you finally get to a point in your life where you can settle down with a companion—that's the stage I'm at now—you pay special attention to what things are about, what life is about."

The couple continued attending weekend services and then enrolled in a marriage preparation seminar at the church. In the course of the seminar, Jarrett and Marlo found out that there were seeker small groups for those who were interested in learning more about Christianity. "We wanted more information, more perspective," says Jarrett. The couple decided to join a group.

Reflecting on the four months he and Marlo have now attended a seeker small group, Jarrett uses words like "safe," "understanding," "convicting," and "educational" to describe the group. "I've learned a lot about applying the Bible to the real world," says Jarrett, who lost his job during the time he's been in the group. "But what really got me is the sensitivity of the people in the group, especially the leaders. It's almost like a small family, a real tight bond."

Ernie and Ginny Johnson are the leaders Jarrett speaks of so highly. "They have great passion," he says. "They're very excited. It's amazing to see that kind of compassion, conviction, from somebody who wants to convey to others what Christ can do in their lives." Jarrett and Marlo have also spent time with the Johnsons outside of the group. "We've had lunch and special times with them," says Jarrett. "They're supportive of us in every way. When we asked them to help us pick out some scriptures for our wedding, they were so excited and honored just to be asked to do that. It's amazing that there are people like this out there. With all the negative news and things going on in your life, you don't realize that there are people who really do care and are willing to help."

When asked what he would say to someone considering whether or not to join a small group, Jarrett is unequivocal. "I highly encourage people to get involved. Give things a fair chance and check it out. It's amazing the people you can meet and the relationships that you can grow in."

Background

Since its official founding in 1975, Willow Creek Community Church has grown from a few hundred young adults in a rented movie theater, to more than sixteen thousand in attendance at weekend services held on its own 145-acre campus in a suburb just outside of Chicago, Illinois. The church's success in pursuing its singular mission, "turning irreligious people into fully devoted followers of Christ," pioneered a "seeker-targeted" approach that has redefined the very nature of the church for some. Over the years, Willow Creek's phenomenal growth has also posed a unique challenge. How does a church of thousands effectively care for and disciple its members? Throughout its development, Willow Creek has responded to this challenge in different ways.

"Back in the early eighties Willow Creek began what I would call a closed-group discipleship model," explains Bill Donahue,[9] executive director of Small Group Ministries at the Willow Creek Association.[10] Because so many in the church had little or no background in Christianity, the central aim of groups in the early years was on education and leadership training. "The primary focus was to understand certain issues about the faith, to develop spiritual disciplines, and to learn how to walk with God," says Donahue. "Participants went to a group for about two-and-a-half years. At the end of that time you were expected to either lead a group just like that or to serve on a ministry team somewhere, but you were never part of a small group again."

While this approach was effective in helping new believers establish roots in the faith, which was a key need at the time, Donahue acknowledges its limitations as the church continued to grow. "It became clear in the late eighties and early nineties that Willow Creek was experiencing the pain of not being able to give enough pastoral care, not keeping people, not shepherding the people who were serving, and leaders [were] burning out." Commenting on the circumstances that prompted development of Willow Creek's current model, Donahue admits, "I'd like to say it was this wonderful, strategically designed kind of thing where we sat down and read the Scriptures and said, 'Ah, look! Community, small groups, we need to start developing that!'

Instead, it was more, 'Ah! We need *help!*' "To address the need, Senior Pastor Bill Hybels and church elders hired a team, including Donahue, Greg Hawkins, and Brett Eastman.

In 1992 this team began to experiment with two new kinds of small groups, what Donahue describes as "community groups" and "task-based groups." Community groups were, for the most part, traditional home-based groups devoted to Bible study and getting people connected to one another. Task-based groups took existing ministry teams and reorganized them into a small-group format so that, for example, ministry teams that formerly just ushered together, now also met for Bible study and mutual support. When these new kinds of groups were launched, Donahue estimates that the church already had 150 to 200 discipleship groups, accounting for 1,500 to 2,000 participants. When the church conducted a survey of members participating in the new groups one year later, a significant number of people named participation in the group as a decisive factor in attending the church. "Five hundred people in that survey said that, had it not been for a connection to a small group, they would have left or considered leaving," says Donahue. "That was new data and it was great to have. People were saying that they felt pastored and connected and so they wanted to stay."

Based in part on the success of these initial groups, Bill Hybels and church leaders made a radical decision. Adapting the meta-church model developed by church consultant Carl George, Willow Creek decided to restructure the entire church based on small groups. "We started to work it from the top down," Donahue explains. "The elders became a small group, the board of directors became several small groups, the management team began to function as a small group prior to its meeting." Although the decision was made in 1993, Donahue points out that it took more than three years to complete the most intensive phase of reorganization. "It was not an easy transition," he recalls. "Some ministries, particularly the children's ministry and the heavily task-oriented ministries needed special treatment." When the reorganization was complete, every department and ministry in the church—from preschoolers to pastors—was rooted in small groups. By 1999 Willow Creek had two thousand small groups representing nearly fifteen thousand small-group participants.

The change signaled a shift in Willow Creek's ministry philosophy. "It's the priesthood of all believers," Donahue points out. "We wanted to release and empower more laity to do ministry." Noting the implications of such a philosophy for the church's budget, he adds, "It's a multimillion-dollar issue here because it means we're putting our resources into people who can build into others who will do the ministry, versus hiring someone to do the ministry." Elaborating on the change, Donahue describes how the transition impacted the responsibilities of church staff: "The number of staff who spend the majority of their time in small-group development and leader development has grown from perhaps a dozen to well over one hundred."

Model Distinctives

The fundamental concept of the meta-church, the model on which Willow Creek is based, is change. Explaining the meaning of the word itself, Carl George writes, "The prefix *meta-* means 'change,' as in *meta*bolism, *meta*morphosis, *meta*physical, and the Greek word *metanoia* ('to change one's mind' or 'repent')."[11] In George's framework, the meta-church is one whose leaders understand and capitalize on change: "A Meta-Church pastor understands how a church can be structured so that its most fundamental spiritual and emotional support centers never become obsolete, no matter how large it becomes overall."[12] At Willow Creek, five key meta-church principles undergird small-group life and church ministry: (1) limited span of care, (2) intentional leadership development, (3) relational discipleship, (4) the open chair, and (5) ministry coordination.

1. *Limited span of care.* Based on the wisdom of Moses' father-in-law, Jethro, who helped Moses to establish a workable means of governing and caring for his people, George articulates a Jethro principle for meta-church pastoral care. "The span-of-care structure that Carl [George] put in place—that everyone is cared for, and no one cares for more than ten—revolutionized Willow Creek," says Bill Donahue. "That basic principle starts with Bill Hybels and the management team, the elders and the board of directors, and works its way down through the entire church. It has allowed us to shepherd people in healthy, pro-active ways instead of just doing 'damage control' because we had too many people to worry about or to try to keep up with."[13] At a structural level, this means group members are cared for by a lay leader, and small group leaders are cared for by lay coaches. "There are about 450 to 500 coaches," says Donahue, "and each one shepherds four to five small group leaders." Coaches, in turn, fall under the care of staff members called division leaders. "At a recent church staff meeting, Bill Hybels asserted that if we had learned nothing else from meta, span-of-care alone was worth the gamble," Donahue relates. "It's reorganized the way we shepherd each other and kept people fresh in ministry."

2. *Intentional leadership development.* George's model stipulates that every leader throughout the meta-church structure should have an apprentice, and all leaders should be thoroughly trained. Embracing this concept at Willow Creek has resulted in a host of leadership training opportunities. The key event each fall is a two-day, off-site leadership retreat, which is no small feat considering that more than 3,500 people attended the most recent one. "The entire leadership of the church is there—all staff, coaches, all the small-group leaders and apprentices," Donahue explains. "It's the leadership body of Willow Creek together, celebrating what God is doing and catching a vision for what this current ministry year will look like." In addition to the retreat, there is a winter conference for coaches, classroom-

based courses on various leadership issues, and a quarterly leadership update cassette tape distributed to every leader. "Put all of that under the umbrella of what we do to support leaders through centralized training," says Donahue. "In addition, the individual ministries are investing in their leaders with ongoing training and encouragement. We really have a lot coming at our leaders, and we ask a lot of them, but we try to invest more in them than we ask of them. That's our goal."

3. *Relational discipleship.* Though the term "discipleship" has often been defined as an intentional relationship between two people, "discipleship" in the meta-model is communal. "It's not just one-on-one discipleship, it's group-based discipleship," Donahue affirms. Drawing on the example of Christ who, as Scripture records, rarely met extensively with fewer than three of the disciples, group-based discipleship "allows disciples to grow in Christ by experiencing the teaching, mentoring, love, encouragement, exhortation, and giftedness of many brothers and sisters in Christ."[14]

4. *The open chair.* The concept of the "open chair" affirms the necessity of making sure the church remains a vital and welcoming body. Carl George states unequivocally, "Show me a nurturing group not regularly open to new life, and I will guarantee that it's dying."[15] By maintaining a posture of openness to new people, the group is enabled to welcome others and grow to the point of eventually "birthing" a new group. Though launching new groups is a goal of the small-groups ministry, it isn't always easy to do. "Our culture is so fragmented that when people finally find six or eight people that they want to do life with, the prospect of breaking that up terrifies them," Donahue explains. "What we try to show them is that by raising up an apprentice leader or two and commissioning them to lead similar kinds of groups, the original group is enabling even more people to experience the very kind of community that has become so important to them."

5. *Ministry coordination.* In the meta-model, the ministries of the church are not a collection of independent programs organized under the umbrella of the local church, but an integrated whole sharing common goals. "It provides a way of structuring and organizing the church so we are all accomplishing the same purpose," Donahue says. "We don't want to merely be a collection of sub-ministries trying to connect to each other. This is the Body of Christ, the Church, so let's act that way!"[16]

Types of Groups

All groups at Willow Creek are rooted in the five values stated above, but there are several ways that the general purposes of the groups themselves are defined. Willow Creek's five major types of groups include community groups, serving groups, seeker groups, support groups, and interest-based groups.

1. *Community groups.* These groups are closest to a traditional understanding of a small group. "This is a home-based kind of group that gathers to study the Bible, learn from the Scriptures, and apply those truths to their lives," Donahue explains. Typically organized by relational affinity within geographic regions, such groups often coalesce around the life-stage of participants—couples, singles, senior adults, and so on.

2. *Serving groups.* The gathering point for serving groups is the accomplishment of a task. With every possible ministry at the church staffed by volunteers, Willow Creek boasts a large number of such "task-based" service groups. In addition to running the church's bookstore, guiding traffic before and after services, working in the inner-city, and staffing the food court, just to name a few, volunteers who serve together also do life together in small groups.

3. *Seeker groups.* Led by believers, seeker small groups provide a safe place for nonbelievers to ask questions and investigate Christianity. The curriculum for the groups is typ-

ically determined by the questions of the group members themselves. According to Donahue, Willow Creek currently has more than fifty seeker small groups.

4. *Support groups.* Support groups generally fall under the pastoral care ministries of the church and are designed for individuals struggling with a specific issue. Groups assist participants with issues such as grief recovery, crisis pregnancy, divorce recovery, weight loss, marriage restoration, and recovery from various addictions.

5. *Interest-based groups.* Affinity for a specific interest such as sports, computers, or a desire to be a better parent gathers many into groups. But being affinity-based doesn't mean the groups aren't outreach oriented. "We have groups for people who like to repair cars," Donahue elaborates. "There are eleven small groups in the CARS ministry. Last year they gave away more than eighty automobiles to people who needed them, and made more than three hundred benevolent repairs. Since the ministry began it has donated more than six hundred cars to people in need."

Looking Ahead

Looking to the future, Willow Creek anticipates few changes in its small-group model. "We're learning to tweak things here and there, but the core components will remain for the foreseeable future," Donahue affirms. Rather, the challenges the church hopes to tackle revolve around two of its core values, leadership and evangelism. "We only have about one-third of our groups that have an official apprentice leader," Donahue explains. "We want to be more intentional about raising up new generations of leaders." In terms of evangelism, Willow Creek intends to emphasize the importance of filling the open chair with unchurched people so evangelism is a high priority in every group, not just seeker groups. "We want to go from fifteen thousand to twenty thousand in small groups by the end of the year 2000," Donahue says. "It's not an arbitrary number; it represents what we believe to be a stewardship of the resources we've been given. That's one of our primary goals. It's going to take everything that we have."

Willow Creek's vision for small groups extends beyond its own campus. The Willow Creek Association has held training conferences on small groups in Australia and New Zealand, and in 1999 held its first small-groups conference in the United States, which attracted more than 1,800 attendees. Speaking of their reasons for holding small-groups conferences, Donahue explains, "The impetus behind this is to help catalyze a movement that we believe God is in. Not that we are the only leaders of it, but it seems that the time is right for Willow Creek to champion that cause and say that this is a place that you can come if you believe that small group ministry is vital to the local church."

• • • • • • •

Our next model is the mission model pioneered by the Church of the Saviour and its founders, Gordon and Mary Cosby. The amazing story of Church of the Saviour was first brought to the attention of many by the writings of church member Elizabeth O'Connor. Among O'Connor's nine books rooted in the life of the church are these classics: *Journey Inward, Journey Outward; The New Community; Letters to Scattered Pilgrims;* and *Cry Pain, Cry Hope.*

Church of the Saviour
Washington, D.C.

Our doctrine from the beginning was deeply orthodox. Our methods were anything that would work. That was what enabled us to dream.

—Mary Cosby,
co-founder, the Church of the Saviour

Don McClanen, Member of a Mission Group

In 1954, Don McClanen, a teacher and athletic director at a small college in Kansas City, Missouri, founded the Fellowship of Christian Athletes (FCA).[17] As the fellowship began to grow, McClanen found himself crisscrossing the country in support of FCA's ministry. Throughout his travels, he started to notice the recurring mention of a unique church in Washington, D.C. "Everywhere I went in those years it was uncanny the way I would hear the Church of the Saviour referred to without ever asking about it," recalls McClanen, now in his seventies.[18] Intrigued by all that he heard, McClanen decided to check out the church for himself. "I took ten days to come to the Church of the Saviour to see if it could be for real," he says. "After three days I called my wife and said, 'Honey, I think we've found our home.'" In 1961, the same year of the visit, Don and Gloria McClanen sold their modest house in Kansas City and moved to Washington, D.C. to join the Church of the Saviour.

Though the couple had been active in a small-group Bible study in the Presbyterian church they attended before moving, McClanen is quick to point out what he considers the critical differences between that group and the mission groups he and Gloria uprooted their lives to be a part of at the Church of the Saviour. "A mission group," he explains, "is more challenging, more demanding, more empowering than a study group. In a mission group we don't just study and pray together, we hold one another accountable. We discuss all of the issues of our lives, such as our money, our values, our family, our total life in Christ." In McClanen's view, the fundamental distinction between the two kinds of groups is one of purpose, why the group comes together in the first place. Whereas the traditional Bible study gathers for spiritual information and mutual support, the mission group gathers for spiritual transformation and ministry outreach. "We are *on* mission," McClanen emphasizes, "we are

Christ's missionaries to the world. Everything is based on the call of a person to mission."

The McClanens' first call to mission took them to DaySpring, the church's retreat farm twenty-five miles northwest of Washington, D.C., in Germantown, Maryland. In 1973, the couple founded a new mission, an experiential seminar and retreat ministry located on DaySpring property. "WellSpring is a mission that shares the lifestyle and commitments of the Church of the Saviour with people from churches across the country and around the world," McClanen explains. "People come here for four to eight days at a time to learn about the inward journey of prayer and meditation, and outward journey of mission." In recent years, McClanen's mission has been devoted to the Ministry of Money, a mission group "that's dealing with the issue of economics and the injustices, materialism, consumerism, and greed of our day."

As he approaches forty years at the Church of the Saviour, McClanen has no doubts about the impact of the church on his life. "It has changed me from an *individual* Christian to a *corporate* Christian," he states. "In a mission group, two or more persons are called of God to the same mission, whether it be housing, or world peacemaking, or hunger, or homelessness. That makes me a corporate Christian rather than just an individual Christian."

Background

As the daughter of a Southern Baptist minister, Mary Cosby grew up in Virginia, and first met her future husband, Gordon, when she was ten and he was fifteen. "The two of us grew up together in Bible Belt Protestantism," Cosby says.[19] "Through all of those years of our growing up, we began to dream wild dreams about church because church was our milieu." Married in 1942, the couple had to put their dreams of starting a church on hold until 1946 when World War II ended and Gordon returned home from his service as a military chaplain.

"It began like a party," says Cosby, recalling the earliest days of the church. "We didn't have any deadlines and we didn't have anybody to look after. We got together with people from my father's church and we borrowed people from our family to talk about it. We began meeting around good restaurants and good food. That went on for about a year, from 1946 to 1947. We had a wonderful time." After gathering a small band of eight to ten, the emergent church began meeting on the front pews of Cosby's father's large church in Alexandria, Virginia, "to talk about our commitment and to write our disciplines and the things that were important to us," Cosby says. "Then we discovered we needed a place to meet." Borrowing on life insurance policies, the group bought a former rooming house for $19,000 and was creative in making repairs. "The walls had broken plaster," Cosby remembers. "We couldn't afford to have it replastered so my mother painted wisteria vines over the broken plaster—it was just beautiful." The Church of the Saviour was officially founded in 1947.

From the beginning, the church had two principles. "One was that it needed to be interracial," Cosby states. "We didn't know how to do that, but we knew that it was a principle of importance." The second principle was what Cosby terms "an integrity of membership." "We wanted there to be a training period for people who came into the faith so they would know exactly what they were saying 'yes' to." Acting on this principle, the church created a spiritual formation program called the School of Christian Living, which persists to this day. "The School of Christian Living is a vital necessity for the training of persons to *be church*," Cosby affirms. "We discovered that the strength of the church was rooted in that." The School of Christian Living curriculum was—and is—a prerequisite to church membership that featured five, ten-week courses: Old Testament, New Testament, Christian doctrine, Christian ethics, and Christian growth. Though formal membership in the church remained small, the school rapidly outgrew its facilities. "Very soon we had over a hundred and then we had a waiting list. It was remarkable how much people wanted it," Cosby recalls. Shortly thereafter, the church purchased a second building to function as both the headquarters for the school and a chapel for worship.

"After the School of Christian Living was running, and we got our building together, and we really began to *be church,* we realized that God was calling us to mission," Cosby says. "The first call of the church came about when a woman put her total retirement fund on Gordon's desk and said, 'This is for the retreat farm fund.' And he said, 'We don't even have fifteen members and we owe $100,000 because we just refurbished our building. A retreat farm is not practical.' The woman replied, 'Well, that's what it's for.' It was *call.* Therefore, it was unanimous. We decided we *did* need a retreat farm—that is our DaySpring House—and it made no sense." The church paid $34,000 for 180 acres in Germantown, Maryland. One year later when the Federal Atomic Energy Commission relocated a mile away, property values skyrocketed. Had the church not purchased the property when it did, it would never have been able to do so. "That's when we learned one of the principles of our church," Cosby reflects, "that sometimes dreams which are not at all rational, when they are based in prayer in a church, often turn out to have the wind of the Holy Spirit in them."

The DaySpring retreat farm is what the church considers an "inward journey" mission. "From the beginning it has been a place of silent retreat," Cosby explains, "but it was not easy for Bible Belt Protestants who talked a lot and who didn't know about silence to realize that they needed to explore depth prayer. So we began to learn from the Catholics and the Quakers—they taught us more about silence than anybody else." Rooted in ever-deeper experiences of prayer, the church discerned another vital principle. "We began to realize that rather than organizing what was needed in the church by forming committees and such, we waited for the call of God," Cosby states. "Our church is built first of all around prayer."

The seeds for the church's second call to mission were planted in 1958. Gordon had been invited to speak at a pre-Lenten service in upstate New York. "It was really not a very happy experience," says Mary Cosby of the service. "It was freezing cold that spring, and the people in the church weren't very friendly because they were all so cold." Beginning their trip back to Washington, D.C. that evening, the couple stopped for the night at a country hotel in Pennsylvania. "It was about midnight," Cosby recalls, "and we heard music and laughter and camaraderie, very noisy but very joyful, coming from a tavern right below us while we were trying to sleep. I remember my husband turned to me and he said, 'If the Lord Jesus were to come back tonight, where do you think he would be more comfortable—in that church we were in this morning, or in the tavern downstairs?' That's when we got the idea that the church had what the tavern didn't have, and the tavern had what the church didn't have. We needed a place that was warm and conversational, and where people knew Jesus Christ. Elizabeth O'Connor described it as a place where 'non-religious people could ask religious questions.' " The resulting mission was a coffeehouse called Potter's House, the church's first outward journey mission, which began in 1960 and is still in operation today. "Potter's House was our first mission to the city," explains Cosby, "and from then on we realized that one of our principles must be to be present in the city and among the poor."

Today, the Church of the Saviour has seventy-three separate missions, from literacy programs and low-income housing, to drug rehabilitation centers and a hospital for the homeless. Though some of the missions require professional staff, all of them have at the center of their operations the mission small group that started the ministry. The Church of the Saviour itself has also multiplied. It operates now as several congregations scattered around the Washington, D.C. area. "In 1976 we realized that the intimacy of our fellowship was going downhill," Cosby says. "The bigger we got, the less effective we were, and fewer missions came about. The smaller we were, the more effective we were." In response, the church took a risky step. "We opened our hands and said, 'Now let us divide ourselves as God calls us to move out from this central focus of being one church, and allow our clusters of missions to become more than one church,' " Cosby recalls. "Within one year six little churches came into being, and now we have ten." *All of the churches are led by laity.* Except for an administrator who assists founding pastor Gordon Cosby, the central church itself has no official staff. Each of the church's seventy-three missions is run by the mission small group that founded it, and they secure paid staff as needed to run the mission.

Looking back on more than fifty years of ministry, Cosby emphasizes the importance of the church's failures as well as its successes. "A very important principle is the need to embrace failure," Cosby insists. "Just about everything we've learned, we've learned by first doing it wrong. You've got to know how to fail and you can't let your people get bogged down into feeling like they're wasting money if it doesn't work out. When people come to visit us and say, 'This is wonderful! How did you come up with this ministry?' we tell them that this is about our hundredth try."

Model Distinctives

In the early years, the Church of the Saviour experiment-ed with various kinds of groups—study groups, prayer groups, fellowship groups—but all of them ultimately failed to thrive. They were what Cosby calls "one-dimensional" groups. "In a one-dimensional group people would, for example, pray very well together for a year or two," Cosby says. "Then when they would decide that they needed to move out in ministry, they would pray for God's direction and God would say, 'Very good, I hear your prayer, but I want *you* to work with children; I want *you* to go to the slums; I want *you* to go to India,' and the whole group got divided up anyway." With this realization, the focus of group development shifted decisively to the primacy of mission. "After long, extended efforts to work with sharing groups, prayer groups, fellowship groups, study groups, on and on, we discovered the necessity of gathering a group first around a common and a corporate mission," Cosby explains. "Then such a multidimensional group became in addition a prayer group, a study group, and all the others as well. This enabled the inward journey of prayer and growth, and the outward journey of mission to happen simultaneously." The Church of the Saviour's definition of such a multidimensional group is eloquently summarized in Gordon Cosby's *Handbook for Mission Groups* as a "small group of people (five to twelve) conscious of the action of the Holy Spirit in their lives, enabling them to hear the call of God through Christ, to belong in love to one another, and to offer the gift of their corporate life for the world's healing and unity."[20]

"The first thing is the call," says Mary Cosby of the manner in which mission groups are formed. When an individual feels that God has placed in his or her heart a dream for a specific ministry, this is the beginning of a call. After discussing the prompting with wise friends and the pastor, the "dreamer of the dream" presents the call to the congregation on a Sunday morning. "A person will stand up at the end of the service and say, 'I feel that something needs to be done in this area. I don't know how to do it, but the call of God to me is to do something about it. If you would be interested in such a group, meet me after church.' That's where mission groups are formed." At this point, some calls are affirmed and some are not. "Sometimes many people respond," says Cosby, "other times, nobody comes and you just have to keep dreaming dreams." When at least two or three respond with commitment, the group accepts the visionary's call as their own and they are ready to take the next step.

"The second thing is the evoking of the gifts," says Cosby, "deciding who is going to do what." By "gifts" Cosby means discerning who in the group is gifted to function in each of the three roles a mission group requires. "To start a group," Cosby continues, "you have to have the caller of the dream, a spiritual director, and a pastor/prophet." The "caller of the dream," sometimes called a "prior" or "moderator," provides inspirational leadership, keeping the group focused on the realization of the vision. The spiritual director cares for the group's spiritual formation and promotes accountability. "Every member gives a spiritual report," Cosby explains, "saying what the week has been like as far as the disciplines are concerned. They ask for prayer, or for whatever they need, and they give that report to the spiritual director so that things don't go undealt [with] within a group." The pastor/prophet's responsibilities sometimes overlap with that of the spiritual director. "The pastor is a shepherd," Cosby states. "The pastor is the one who is in touch with people who need ministering to, who need comfort, or laughter . . . that person also helps to hold people accountable." With these three roles established, "you can get all the extra gifts that people have, like music, teaching, painting—all those things can be used," says Cosby. "But you have to first have those three before you can be considered a mission group of this church."

The group then enters into a time of prayer and self-education to further discern the shape and structure of its mission. Though all group members have completed the School of Christian Living, most find that they are called to missions that exceed their current knowledge or skills. "We never have an expert called to open a mission," Cosby states. "For instance, we've never had a brilliant schoolteacher called to work in the educational system." Though professionals often will join the group at a later stage, Cosby believes experts rarely sound the call for mission because, "they know how hard it is and that it will cost their lives." Rather, visionaries are more often those who don't know what they can't do. "We always say that our people are like the biblically called people who say, 'I don't know how to do it, Lord.' But, they get educated. The group educates itself, and part of the discipline is the study around the mission." As the group's process continues, it will eventually collaborate on a carefully crafted mission statement to outline its purpose and goals, and formalize its ministry structure.

The mission of a group may persist for decades—as have the church's first two missions, DaySpring and Potter's House—or they may end when the mission project is complete. And calls for certain individuals may change. "I was in the Potter's House mission group for thirteen years before I made a change," says Cosby. "The groups are always open to change because, as one of the members said to me, 'You're not a gift to the group if you're not called, and you're not a gift to yourself if you're not called to the group.' So it works very well."

Looking Ahead

When asked about the future plans and direction for the church, Cosby responds philosophically. "I don't think we really know. We simply have to be open to what God will call us to. I don't think any of us is called to perpetuity—for us to lay down something is as good as picking up the next thing. We don't have organizational needs which have got to be held onto, so we are open to whatever the Lord leads us to do." As she considers the future, Cosby also reflects on the past. "There is no denying that within the past fifty years God's power has been at work among this fragile community, and it is fragile," Cosby emphasizes. "We fall in the pits all the time, and you can find every major problem in our people that you find in any cross section of people." Nevertheless, Cosby affirms, "Those of us who have gathered as mission groups of our church have been aware of two things. One, the weakness and fragility of our little community; and two, the astounding action of God using us in spite of ourselves."

• • • • • • •

Located thousands of miles west of Washington, D.C. in Anaheim, California, is a church that would also affirm the astounding action of God in their midst. Founded by John Wimber, a jazz musician turned pastor, this charismatic church began as a small group that worshiped and prayed together in a home. Throughout its development, and despite challenges and setbacks, home groups have remained a central feature of Vineyard Christian Fellowship.

Vineyard Christian Fellowship
Anaheim, California

"Everybody gets to do the stuff."
—*John Wimber, founding pastor,*
Vineyard Christian Fellowship

Lisa Hughey, Leader of a Home Group

Lisa Hughey, a thirty-eight-year-old kindergarten teacher, was reared in the Lutheran faith but came of age during the heyday of the Southern California revival movement launched by Chuck Smith, founder of Calvary Chapel. During her years as a college student at California State Polytechnic University in Pomona, she was actively involved in Campus Crusade for Christ as a leader and short-term mission participant. After college, Hughey joined a large evangelical church in Southern California where she became a small-group leader. Though she was committed to the church and her group, over time she began to feel like something was missing.

"I was really burning out with the traditional small-group Bible study," says Hughey, recalling the journey that eventually brought her to Vineyard Christian Fellowship in Anaheim, California, in 1987.[21] "There was a lack of true fel-

71

lowship, of vulnerability, of accountability and confession of sin. There was a lot of surface stuff . . . very rarely would you talk about things in your personal life that might be going wrong, or have people pray for you at that level." When a college friend mentioned that she knew of a great small group in their area, Hughey accepted an invitation to check it out.

Hughey's first experience of a Vineyard home group proved decisive. "People were very loving and the level of discussion was much deeper than I was used to," she recalls. When she shared personal concerns, group members laid hands on her and prayed for her. Group leaders expressed genuine interest and demonstrated a willingness to help in any way they could. Drawn by the intimacy and care she experienced, Hughey kept coming back. "Their absolute love and acceptance had a profound impact on me," she recalls. "I was coming out of church and parachurch experiences in which you did not get input if you did not have output. If you weren't moving, growing, ministering, there was no time for you. This was a very different experience in that I could just be 'nobody' and I was treated with tremendous respect, tremendous love." Six months after her first visit to a Vineyard home group, Hughey became a member of the church.

Reflecting on the impact that Vineyard has had on her life, Hughey, now a home-group leader herself, first cites the transparency and confession modeled by small-group leaders and pastors. "John Wimber floored me," she says of the church's late founder. "I had never sat under a pastor who would talk about things that he was struggling with in his personal life. It gave me the freedom to share things that I was struggling with, to bring them out into the light and let people pray for me." Deep friendships and mentoring relationships resulted from such shared vulnerability, as well as a more powerful experience of prayer and answers to prayer. And the home group provided a safe and instructive environment for Hughey to develop her spiritual gifts. "I've learned to minister in many different ways in the small groups I've been in," she explains. "One of them was learning how to use the more miraculous gifts like word of knowledge, healing, tongues. . . . For the first time, I could actually practice using [my] gifts on other people where there was modeling, immediate feedback, and encouragement. It was an eye-opening, life-changing experience."

Background

Before John Wimber became a Christian, the Vineyard's founding pastor was a professional musician and original member of the Righteous Brothers. Converted through the ministry of a fellow band member in 1963, John and his wife, Carol, spent their early years in the faith as members of a Quaker congregation. In 1971, Wimber became a pastor and joined the staff of Yorba Linda Friends Church in Southern California, where he and Carol had been active members. Three years later in 1974, Wimber left the pastorate to accept C. Peter Wagner's invitation to become founding director of the Charles E. Fuller Institute of Church Growth at Fuller Theological Seminary in Pasadena, a post he held until 1978. At the same time he was at Fuller, Wimber began to become involved with Chuck Smith's Calvary Chapel movement.

"In the mid-seventies, John and a core group of ten to twelve people—partly his relatives and partly his friends—started to have what they called 'after-glow' meetings at a person's home," says Vineyard associate pastor Van Pewthers, recalling the beginnings of the church as a home-based small group.[22] "They were looking for a deeper, more personal, and intimate relationship with the Lord." As part of their meetings, the group worshiped and sang together. "They found that singing helped calm and focus their hearts," says Pewthers of the worship style that would become a Vineyard hallmark, "and certain types of songs caused them to have a sense of God's presence in a very special way." On Mother's Day in 1977, the group held its first service as Calvary Chapel of Yorba Linda with 150 people in attendance and John Wimber as pastor.

By 1978, one year after its first service, Calvary Chapel of Yorba Linda had nearly doubled in size, though its most spectacular growth would come over the next two years. "John was really beginning to have some influence because of some things the Lord had shown him about the works of the Kingdom," Pewthers says, commenting on what prompted the church's phenomenal growth. "The Lord began to back up some of his teaching about healing with people actually getting healed." When Wimber then began teaching a course on "signs and wonders" at Fuller, "people that were taking the class started getting healed," Pewthers says. "Suddenly there was a lot of interest in what was going on. The church went from about 250 to, two years later, close to 5,000 people."

The church became increasingly influenced by its experience of what Pewthers terms "manifestational giftings"—miraculous spiritual gifts such as prophecy, words of knowledge and wisdom, healing, and tongues—and developed an emphasis on the public use of the gifts of the Holy Spirit that resulted in the church's formal separation from Calvary Chapel in the early 1980s. Joining with a handful of like-minded fellowships that were organized by Kenn Gulliksen in 1974 under the name "Vineyard," the merged groups held their first official church service as Vineyard Christian Fellowship of Anaheim in 1982. Under Wimber's leadership, the movement grew to more than four hundred congregations in the United States and another two hundred worldwide.[23]

As the church grew, so did the number of small groups. "When there were 250 people in the church we had maybe 7 or 8 small groups," Pewthers recalls. "We went from that to about 120 to 175 small groups" when the church grew to almost 5,000. Sunday corporate worship and weekly small-group meetings were the two arenas for everything that happened in the church. "In the initial stages, all of our evangelism, all of our ministries to the poor, everything was handled through the small-group environment," Pewthers explains. "John Wimber's vision was really for an *empowered laity*. . . . As he used to say, 'Everybody gets to do the stuff,' meaning the stuff of the Kingdom." Elaborating on the vital role of home groups in the formative years of the church, Pewthers states, "The small group was where leadership got developed, where people got connected with one another, and where they got to test their gifting—to experiment, if you will, with being able to lay hands on one another, and to offer words of knowledge, and words of wisdom."

The remarkable success of Vineyard catapulted Wimber onto the national scene and prompted a number of new ventures. Between 1981 and 1985, the church recorded and released two albums of worship music, started a training conference center called Vineyard Ministries International, initiated a magazine called *First Fruits*,[24] formed a recording company called Mercy Records, began a publishing operation called Mercy Media, and incorporated the Association of Vineyard Churches. By 1986 there were two hundred Vineyard churches across the country and around the world.[25]

At the same time, Wimber began to travel extensively, speaking at conferences throughout the United States and internationally. "When he started being gone a great deal of the time," Pewthers recalls, "he put the local church under the leadership of other people [who] believed God wanted them to create a more programmatic infrastructure." The breakneck pace of growth had placed considerable demands on the church's ministries, all of which had previously been conducted through small groups. "We responded to the fact that we were getting bigger by creating programs," Pewthers explains. "Our work with the poor became a program and we put a pastor over it; evangelism became more formalized and we put a pastor over it." Though leaders couldn't see it at the time, the shift in ministry structure dealt a serious blow to the vitality of the church's small groups. "Small groups became in essence a kind of competing program," says Pewthers. "We didn't see it at the time, but [the programs] started sapping the strength of the small groups." When the dust cleared, the number of small groups had declined to around thirty.

In the early 1990s, the church had come to grips with the decline in its home groups and was beginning to reemphasize them when it was rocked with the news in 1993 that its founder and senior pastor had been diagnosed with cancer. Two years later, Wimber suffered a stroke and subsequently installed as senior pastor Carl Tuttle, who served in that role until June 1997. On November 17, 1997, John Wimber died of a massive brain hemorrhage.

Pewthers describes the Anaheim Vineyard today as "a church in transition." Attendance of adults is three thousand and the number of home groups has rebounded to fifty. Shortly after being installed in 1997, the church's senior pastor, Lance Pittluck, signaled his dedication to revitalizing the home-group ministry by personally starting and leading a group. In 1998 he charged Van Pewthers, a member of the church since 1978 and a pastor on staff, with the responsibility of charting a new course for Vineyard's small-group ministry. "My vision for the home groups is that they be little churches," says Pewthers. "Small groups are the place where we are radically impacted by the gospel because we see the works of the Kingdom, we get to know one another in self-revealing ways, and we learn how to apply the gospel."

Model Distinctives

The organizational structure for Vineyard home groups begins with associate pastor Van Pewthers, and assistant pastor for home groups, Michelle English, the two staff members charged with running the ministry. Pewthers and English work directly with twelve regional oversight leaders, who in turn each oversee approximately five home-group leaders. Regional oversight leaders are laypersons who have proven themselves as effective home-group leaders capable of training and releasing upcoming leaders to start new groups. Unlike the traditional small group of fewer than ten people, the fifty Vineyard home groups average between fifteen and twenty participants apiece, and a few run as large as forty-five. When this larger group breaks up into smaller clusters in the course of a meeting, the clusters are led by core-group members. Under the direction of the home-group leader, core-group members are leaders-in-training who assist the home-group leader with every aspect of group life. Regional oversight leaders, home-group leaders, and core-group members comprise the lay leadership structure of Vineyard's small-group ministry.

Generally speaking, the traditional Vineyard home group includes five key elements—fellowship, worship, Scripture teaching, ministry, and outreach. However, Van Pewthers stresses an overriding principle of diversity and flexibility that shapes how each element is expressed within a given group. "Our overall belief is that God loves wondrous variety," Pewthers affirms. "Each of the home groups that we have here is going to be flavored by the vision and giftedness of those who lead." Commenting on the responsibility of those who provide oversight to the ministry, he adds, "Our job is to draw people to a unifying vision that allows the variety that God has built into their hearts to blossom." Keeping in mind the diversity inherent in each gathering, a typical small group meets once a week for two to three hours in a member's home and includes the following elements.

1. *Fellowship.* "We believe that two relationships are key— relationship to God, and relationship to one another," says Pewthers. "Fellowship is getting to know one another and becoming involved in one another's lives." On one level, this is as simple as the casual cookie-and-coffee time that often begins a gathering, or as elaborate as more formal times beyond the meeting when members get together for an outing or social event. On a deeper level, fellowship is forged within the meeting in times of vulnerability when

members share struggles, confess sins, and "bear one another's burdens."

2. *Worship.* In the meeting, worship typically begins with a period of singing, but Vineyard's concept of worship is broader. "Worship has a very special meaning for us," Pewthers explains. "It isn't just singing songs to Jesus, it is establishing intimacy with God." Further clarifying his point, Pewthers adds, "If fellowship is the thrust toward having relationship with one another, worship is the thrust toward having relationship with God, and being open to him and his manifest presence." During worship, this "manifest presence" expresses itself when members of the group share "prophetic words, words of knowledge, or words of encouragement," explains Pewthers. Vineyard also stresses worship as a lifestyle. "We say that we worship in everything that we do," Pewthers says. "Our time, our energy, our monies are really all God's, and we worship God by how we use our time, energy, and money."

3. *Scripture teaching.* In the past, Vineyard has been criticized for what some considered a lack of emphasis on Scripture. Van Pewthers acknowledges the criticism but interprets it as a misunderstanding of the church's teaching that emphasizes "being not only hearers but doers of the word." Within the group meeting, teaching can be as formal as a prepared lesson delivered by the home-group leader or a core-group member, or as informal as a free-form discussion of that week's sermon. Again, all depends on the gifts and skills of the leader. Whatever the format, the Scripture teaching is what assistant pastor Michelle English describes as being "application oriented." "We want people to interact with God's Word," English states. "We want to help people grab hold of it in a way that changes their lives, rather than just giving them more intellectual information."

4. *Ministry.* The ministry portion of the group meeting often begins with intercessory prayer. "We encourage people to intercede on a regular basis for their group and for

the church at large," says Pewthers. "That might mean the Anaheim church, it might mean the Body of Christ in Orange County, or it might mean the mysterious Body of Christ in the United States or the world." The focus then turns to the specific needs of individual group members. After breaking up into clusters of two to five, members share personal concerns and confess struggles and sins. "Then we lay hands on people," says Pewthers. "The small groups are the primary place people get to practice 'doing the stuff,' as John [Wimber] used to say, the stuff of the Kingdom." Sharing specific personal issues facilitates accountability and spiritual care, important features of the group. "If I'm not willing to be open to another," states Pewthers, "then things can continue in my life or take root in my life that are not of God, and they will not get healed or rooted out."

5. *Outreach.* Outreach takes the ministry of group members beyond the confines of the group. "Instead of being self-focused about who we are as a group, outreach focuses on serving the Body of Christ together," says Pewthers. "We supply [the groups] with suggestions on ways they can reach out and serve the poor, for example, or how they can do something in their neighborhood that is evangelistically oriented."

Looking Ahead

Acknowledging that the church is in transition, Van Pewthers looks to the future as a time of creative opportunity. "We're moving back to the primacy of the home groups as the central expression of the church, and so we have the opportunity to reinvent ourselves," he says. Michelle English affirms the primacy of the groups, adding that the model itself is undergoing changes. "We know we want to recapture small groups," she says, "not because it's small groups, but because it is a place of community." Noting that the culture has changed a great deal over the more than twenty years the church has been in existence, English stresses the importance of leaving some elements behind and embracing others. "There are some things that we don't want to recapture," she says, "like having a primary leader do everything, and teaching the Bible strictly in a lecture format." Already, this has prompted the creation of a team concept of shared leadership that has been wholeheartedly embraced by the groups who are pilot-testing it.

According to Pewthers, the church has a goal of adding twenty new groups within the coming year. This has spawned experimental groups that focus, for example, on an interest such as dance and the creative arts, that are structured differently than the traditional model. "We are willing to talk to those who have another model on their heart, and figure out if that fits within the overall small-group thrust that we have here," Pewthers affirms.

Reaching the next generation and training them for leadership make up one of Vineyard's key objectives. "We are very aware of the fact that we have a new generation coming up with different needs. We want to prepare the church to reach them and appropriately change for them," says English. Pewthers agrees, "We have to be flexible enough to raise up the next generation of leaders and it's going to look different. We have to be open to what 'small group' means for them." Acknowledging the high value that Generation X places on relationships and "hanging out," Vineyard has embraced an existing ministry format designed to reach this generation called "Alpha." In the context of a larger gathering, "Alpha breaks down for discussion into small groups that meet around tables. Alpha is providing two different resources for us," English explains. "It's helping us reach the lost, but it's also hands-on training for the table leaders." "Alpha is a big front door," Pewthers adds. "We're using it as a whole new way to generate groups. At the end of the [ten-week] Alpha process, the intention is that the table leaders will transition to home-group leaders and the group will continue meeting. This is a real success story for us."

Though many things may change in Vineyard's methods, Pewthers affirms the core value of everything the church does: "To be fully known, fully empowered, and growing in Christlikeness—this is Christ's heart for his church."

• • • • • • •

Unlike the three previous models, the RENOVARÉ model is not affiliated with one particular church. This is, in fact, a key feature in that one of the model's objectives is to draw together that which is best from several different traditions of the church universal. Founded by Richard J. Foster, author of the bestselling *Celebration of Discipline,* RENOVARÉ is a nonprofit organization and a spiritual formation movement.

RENOVARÉ
Bringing the Church to the Churches

RENOVARÉ (pronounced ren-o-var-a) is a Latin word meaning to renew. The Apostle Paul declares "Though outwardly we are wasting away, yet inwardly we are being renewed (renovaré) day by day" (2 Corinthians 4:16).[26]

Valerie Hess, Member of a
Spiritual Formation Group

Valerie Hess, a forty-four-year-old wife, mother, and professional musician, describes her first exposure to the spiritual disciplines as a crushing weight. After reading Richard Foster's *Celebration of Discipline,* she says, "I was in despair." She found the descriptions of twelve spiritual disciplines meaningful and compelling but had no idea what to do with what she read. How did one assimilate this material and apply it to everyday life? Noting the passages in Matthew 21 and Luke 20 where Jesus alludes to himself as the cornerstone in the kingdom of God, Valerie recalls, "Jesus says that whoever stumbles on the stone will be broken, and whomever the stone falls upon will be crushed. I felt like the spiritual disciplines were a stone that had fallen on me and was about to crush me."[27]

That began to change in 1992 when Valerie discovered RENOVARÉ, a spiritual formation program created by Richard Foster. "I'll never forget it," says Valerie, when asked about her first encounter with the program. "I was upstairs on this little couch that we had in our bedroom at the time. The girls were asleep and John was at a meeting. I was looking at the RENOVARÉ materials, and as I read I was getting more and more excited. I thought to myself, this is it. This is what I have been looking for." Recalling her earlier experience of feeling crushed, Valerie reflects, "RENOVARÉ helped me to break up that huge stone into little bits of gravel."

The organizing principle of the RENOVARÉ curriculum is centered in six great traditions, to which Foster gives the following designations:

Contemplative
Holiness
Charismatic
Social Justice
Evangelical
Incarnational[28]

"By coming to understand something of each tradition, I had a framework that I could plug into," says Valerie. Her next step was to join together with two other women from her church to form a RENOVARÉ spiritual formation group. "I found that I could accomplish something each week by being accountable to Gwen and Kathy," says Valerie. "Vague concepts like righteousness, holiness, and confession, suddenly became very concrete to me," she notes. "That whole concept of loving your enemies is very nice until you have to do it, and then go to your group the next week and talk about how you did." It is precisely this combination of a practical framework for understanding the spiritual life, and the encouragement and accountability of her small group that Valerie Hess credits as transformational.

Background

The creation of RENOVARÉ is intimately connected to the life of its founder, Richard J. Foster. As Foster's first book, *Celebration of Discipline,* rose to the top of the bestseller lists in the early 1980s, Foster was invited by many churches to come and speak about the spiritual disciplines. "It gave me the opportunity to be among Christians of many denominations, various geographic areas, and racial and ethnic backgrounds," Foster explains. "I saw many excellent things everywhere I went, but during those years of travel I also saw three great areas of spiritual deficiency."[29]

First, Foster discerned "that people were trying rather than training." Though Christians wanted to live lives of faithful obedience, Foster likened the spiritual struggles and failures they encountered to one who tries to run a marathon without ever training for it. "They did not understand the importance of spiritual training so that there could be built within them deeply ingrained habits of love and joy, peace and patience, kindness and goodness, faithfulness and gentleness, and self-control."[30]

The second deficiency Foster observed was "that people were scattered rather than gathered." Rather than finding themselves in a community of support and accountability, Christians more often found themselves without spiritual guides or companions. "Even in our churches, if someone seriously intends to be a disciple of Jesus Christ . . . they will find themselves alone and isolated," Foster says. "We were never meant to live the spiritual life alone. God's intention is that we have the support and nurture and loving accountability of other disciples of Jesus."[31]

The third deficiency was "that the vision of the people was myopic rather than synoptic." Noting that those who are raised or converted in certain traditions tend to remain within them, Foster saw that many Christians were cut off from the wisdom of other traditions. "They understood only a thin slice of all that God intended for them," Foster explains. "So their vision is partial, it's been stunted. It is myopic."[32]

These realizations were so distressing that in the summer of 1986 Foster stepped back from all speaking and writing, not knowing at the time if he would ever return to either. "This period lasted for about eighteen months," Foster recalls. "During that time I tried to listen carefully to God. What could be done to overcome these crippling deficiencies?" A decisive turning point came one day when he was out for his afternoon jog, a time in which Foster often sang and prayed. "As I began praying that day, I felt addressed by God, and the whole vision for what we now call RENOVARÉ came tumbling forth—a vision of a freely gathered and spiritually disciplined people who could learn and grow and draw strength from all the great streams of life and faith throughout the history of the people of God."[33]

In 1992 Foster retired from his position as executive director of The Milton Center and professor of theology at Friends University to focus the bulk of his attention on launching RENOVARÉ.

Model Distinctives

In his book *Streams of Living Water,* Foster describes the work of God in our time as drawing together many "streams of the spiritual life" into "a mighty 'Mississippi of the Spirit.'" These streams are what Foster names the six great traditions of the church, and they comprise the foundational core of the RENOVARÉ model. As RENOVARÉ materials describe them, the six traditions are:

- **Contemplative: The Prayer-Filled Life**

  Focuses upon intimacy with God and depth of spirituality. This spiritual dimension addresses the longing for a deeper, more vital Christian experience.

- **Holiness: The Virtuous Life**

  Focuses upon personal moral transformation and the power to develop "holy habits." This spiritual dimension addresses the erosion of moral fiber in personal and social life.

- **Charismatic: The Spirit-Empowered Life**

  Focuses upon the charisms of the Spirit and worship. This spiritual dimension addresses the yearning for the immediacy of God's presence among his people.

- **Social Justice: The Compassionate Life**

  Focuses upon justice and *shalom* in all human relationships and social structures. This spiritual dimension addresses the gospel imperative for equity and compassion among all peoples.

- **Evangelical: The Word-Centered Life**

  Focuses upon the proclamation of the evangel, the good news of the gospel. This spiritual dimension addresses the need for people to see the good news lived and hear the good news proclaimed.

- **Incarnational: The Sacramental Life**

  Focuses upon making present and visible the realm

of the invisible spirit. This spiritual dimension addresses the crying need to experience God as truly manifest
and notoriously active in daily life.[34]

By drawing on what is best from each tradition and utilizing it as the framework for spiritual formation, the RENOVARÉ
model is designed to provide correctives to the three spiritual deficiencies Foster observed. Valerie Hess describes this
aspect of the program as "cross-training in the Spirit," and the
"spiritual equivalent of what diet, exercise, and proper rest is
to the physical life." The focus is restoring balance to spiritual growth and discipleship by reclaiming the "best spiritual
treasures" from each of the six great streams.

RENOVARÉ utilizes newsletters, retreats, resources, and
conferences to carry out its work, but the heart of the
movement is rooted in its spiritual formation groups. A
group is two to eight people who agree to meet regularly,
and who are committed to the RENOVARÉ Covenant, which
says, "In utter dependence upon Jesus Christ as my ever
living Savior, Teacher, Lord, and Friend, I will seek contin-
ual renewal through: spiritual exercises, spiritual gifts, and
acts of service."[35] Rather than identifying one person as
leader, group members rotate leadership from week to
week and share responsibility for facilitating group meetings.

Once a group has formed, members are introduced to
the framework by going through an eight-week study in
A Spiritual Formation Workbook by James Bryan Smith, a
RENOVARÉ board member who serves as chaplain and
assistant professor at Friends University. After an intro-
ductory session that traces the source of each tradition
back to the model of Christ, successive sessions explore
the biblical foundations, history, and practices of the six
traditions.[36] Included in the presentation of each tradition
are a range of spiritual exercises based on that tradition.
Participants choose one of the exercises and commit to
practicing it and then discussing their experience of it

with the group at their next meeting. In this way, members get practical experience in developing spiritual disciplines in every tradition and are supported by other group members in a context of loving accountability. Commenting on the merits of this approach, Dallas Willard, a RENOVARÉ board member, says, "The central value of RENOVARÉ is that it enables people to begin where they are to follow Jesus Christ, concretely, effectively, in a way that is responsible to others around them, without requiring that they already be masters of anything."[37]

The final session outlines the format for continuing the spiritual formation group, and offers specific guidelines to help the group make that transition. The ongoing format for spiritual formation group meetings is outlined in the "Order of Meeting," which begins with the brief recitation of opening words. This statement welcomes participants, reminds them of the purpose of the group, and stresses the importance of confidentiality. Next, the group recites together the RENOVARÉ Covenant. Following the Covenant, group members take turns reading through the RENOVARÉ Common Disciplines. Grounded in the six traditions, the Common Disciplines outline the foundational commitments that members pledge to practice in everyday life.

- **Contemplative: The Prayer-Filled Life**

    By God's grace, I will set aside time regularly for prayer, meditation, and spiritual reading and will seek to practice the presence of God.

- **Holiness: The Virtuous Life**

    By God's grace, I will strive mightily against sin and will do deeds of love and mercy.

- **Charismatic: The Spirit-Empowered Life**

  By God's grace, I will welcome the Holy Spirit, exercising the gifts and nurturing the fruit while living in the joy and power of the Spirit.

- **Social Justice: The Compassionate Life**

  By God's grace, I will endeavor to serve others everywhere I can and will work for justice in all human relationships and social structures.

- **Evangelical: The Word-Centered Life**

  By God's grace, I will share my faith with others as God leads and study the Scriptures regularly.

- **Incarnational: The Sacramental Life**

  By God's grace, I will joyfully seek to show forth the presence of God in all that I say, in all that I do, in all that I am.[38]

The heart of the meeting begins when group members look for "the footprints of God," in their lives, and especially so in regard to the previous week's chosen spiritual discipline or exercise. By reflecting together on victories and challenges alike, members find guidance and encouragement for spiritual training and growth. As a springboard for discussing one's experiences and concerns, small-group participants utilize the Renovaré Questions of Examen for this portion of the meeting.

- **Contemplative: The Prayer-Filled Life**

  In what ways has God made his presence known to you since our last meeting? What experiences of prayer, meditation, and spiritual reading has God given you? What difficulties or frustrations have you encountered? What joys and delights?

- **Holiness: The Virtuous Life**

  What temptations have you faced since our last meeting? How did you respond? Which spiritual disciplines has God used to lead you further into holiness of heart and life?

- **Charismatic: The Spirit-Empowered Life**

  Have you sensed any influence or work of the Holy Spirit since our last meeting? What spiritual gifts has the Spirit enabled you to exercise? What was the outcome? What fruit of the Spirit would you like to see increase in your life? What disciplines might be useful in this effort?

- **Social Justice: The Compassionate Life**

  What opportunities has God given you to serve others since our last meeting? How did you respond? Have you encountered any injustice to or oppression of others? Have you been able to work for justice and *shalom*?

- **Evangelical: The Word-Centered Life**

  Has God provided an opportunity for you to share your faith with someone since our last meeting? How did you respond? In what ways have you encountered Christ in your reading of Scripture? How has the Bible shaped the way you think and live?

- **Incarnational: The Sacramental Life**

In what ways have you been able to manifest the presence of God through your daily work since our last meeting? How has God fed and strengthened you through the ministry of Word and Sacrament?[39]

The questions are intended to provide a framework, not a rigid sieve for poking through the hollows of each one's spiritual life. No participant is expected to answer questions in all six areas, but each is encouraged to answer those that pertain to their exercise from the previous week as a means of reflection and accountability. Commenting on the value of entrusting oneself to the care of a group, James Bryan Smith says, "What these groups do is . . . give people an opportunity to find practical ways to move forward in this endeavor . . . they give local churches a tool by which they can help Christians join together and encourage one another, using the power that comes from mutual accountability and watching over one another in love."[40]

After discussion of the Questions of Examen is complete, group members share the specific exercises they plan to undertake in the coming week. The meeting concludes with the group praying together the Lord's Prayer, and reciting a two-sentence benediction by that week's designated leader.

Looking Ahead

In the near future, RENOVARÉ's plans include continuing or expanding many of the things they are already doing well—creating new resources, publishing newsletters, and conducting regional conferences. Occasionally, RENOVARÉ hopes to also sponsor international conferences, such as the one it held in Houston, Texas, in 1999, which was attended by more than two thousand people. According to Lynda Graybeal, a long-time colleague of Richard Foster and administrator at RENOVARÉ, opportunities may be opening up to establish RENOVARÉ in England, Australia, and countries in western Europe. However, she is quick to add that RENOVARÉ is not in "empire-building mode," and any plans for international expansion will depend heavily on the emergence of others who are willing to champion such an endeavor. Transcending the strategic goals of RENOVARÉ as an organization, is the expansive vision of its founder, Richard Foster:

> I see a day when a Southern Baptist pastor from Alabama embraces an Episcopal priest from New Jersey and together they pray for the peace of the world.
>
> I see a day when evangelicals and social activists weep together over the spiritually lost and the plight of the poor.
>
> I see a day when Methodist prayer warriors join hands with Catholic contemplatives and offer a sacrifice of worship.
>
> I see a day when guileless Sunday school children join with sophisticated theologians and sing "Jesus loves me! This I know, for the Bible tells me so. Little ones to him belong; they are weak, but he is strong."
>
> I see a day when all God's people, from every race and class and category, blend their hearts and voices in song, declaring, "Amazing grace! How sweet the sound that saved a wretch like me! I once was lost, but now am found; was blind, but now I see."[41]

Spurred on by this soul-stirring vision, and undergirded by resources immersed in the great streams of the faith, those who take up the RENOVARÉ discipline will *not only* be transformed, but also will create a world in which Foster's dream may surely be realized.

• • • • • • •

Our final model differs from the previous four in that it is not really a small-group model at all. Rather, a clearness committee is a centuries-old Quaker tradition that offers a framework for communal discernment. Though small groups of all kinds are typically well equipped to deal with the ongoing concerns and struggles of daily life, sometimes individuals face decisions and circumstances requiring special attention. The clearness committee offers an effective means of addressing such concerns and has been particularly significant in my own life.

Clearness Committee
Community for Discernment

The clearness committee can help people discover their own God-given leadings and callings through silence, through questioning, through listening, through prayer.
—*Parker J. Palmer* [42]

Beth Burbank and Bill Esler

Beth Burbank and Bill Esler have a mixed marriage—she is Quaker, he is Roman Catholic. When their son, Kyran, was born, Beth and Bill decided to raise him as a Quaker in Beth's tradition, while simultaneously honoring elements of the Catholic tradition that were important to Bill. For example, while Kyran is a member of the Quaker meeting, he also has godparents, a feature of Catholicism that is absent from the Quaker tradition. Though the decision to have godparents was a fairly simple one, raising a child in a way that honors two religious traditions has also posed some challenging questions.

A recent question revolved around a central feature of Roman Catholic worship—the Eucharist—that is not part of Quaker practice. Kyran, now seven, attends a Catholic school that prepares students for First Communion during second grade. "We had been raising him a Quaker," explains Beth, "but when the issue of communion came up, we had to ask ourselves if it was okay for him to also be Catholic." [43]

To navigate their way through this issue, Beth and Bill relied on an informal adaptation of a time-honored Quaker tradition: the clearness committee. In this case, their "committee" was Kyran's godparents, one of whom was Quaker and one of whom was Catholic. "They helped us sort out the whole process, including Kyran's own input," says Beth. By asking questions, the godparents helped Beth and Bill work through their feelings, beliefs, expectations, concerns, and the implications of their decision. After going back and forth and considering all the issues, one question proved especially helpful. "In the end, the thing that helped us decide was when Kyran's godmother, who is Catholic, asked us if we would [have enrolled] Kyran in CCD class and have him do this if he was not in Catholic school," recalls Beth. "Bill and I both looked at each other and said, 'No, we wouldn't.'" The couple decided to continue raising Kyran as a Quaker, and to allow Kyran, when he is older, to choose whether or not to be baptized to the Catholic faith and take communion.

Background

From their beginnings as a persecuted minority in seventeenth-century England, the Society of Friends, or Quakers as they came to be called, have placed a high value on discernment as an issue of communal significance. This was especially important in the earliest years of the movement when the rash action of one member could initiate indiscriminate retribution on the entire community.[44] Communal oversight also had a very practical expression when Quakers became more established and began releasing members to serve in foreign missions. In one of its earliest expressions, the clearness process provided unmarried individuals who traveled abroad with papers affirming that they were in fact not married. "They would go off to the New World and no one knew them," explains Beth Burbank, a lifelong Quaker. "They would carry with them a letter of introduction and they would receive clearness from their own meeting before they left that stipulated there were no impediments to them getting married."

In more recent usage within the Society of Friends, this process that has come to be called a "clearness committee" has both formal and informal functions. Formal clearness committees revolve around issues of official business or concern to the entire Quaker meeting. Two expressions of the formal clearness committee address requests for membership in the meeting and requests for marriage under the care of the meeting. The clearness committee for membership focuses on making sure that the applicant understands and is "clear" on what it means to be Quaker and how that may impact his or her life. Taking seriously their responsibility to care for those seeking marriage under the care of the meeting, the clearness committee for marriage helps the couple explore their compatibility and readiness for this commitment. In both cases, clearness committees result in recommendations that are presented to the entire meeting for approval. Informal clearness committees, on the other hand, do not typically concern themselves with issues requiring the approval of the entire meeting. Rather, these clearness committees are focused on assisting individuals in addressing issues of personal concern. It is this informal application of the traditional clearness committee that has particular relevance for the contemporary church.

We live in a time when few would disagree that North American culture has become increasingly fragmented. As intentional forms of community life and discourse have grown scarce, even those who have been raised in the church lack models for meaningful and healthy engagement in the lives of their brothers and sisters in Christ. The time-tested model of the clearness committee cannot solve such a pervasive problem on its own, but it does provide a proven means for reconnecting individuals and communities around issues of personal discernment. "As the clearness committee has been evolving, it seems to offer a way back into community support and guidance at critical times in people's lives," writes Patricia Loring. "While functioning as an instrument for discernment, it also helps recover the communal dimension of the spiritual life in relationships, in the vitality and authority that come of profound union in and commitment to God."[45]

Model Distinctives

Quaker author and educator, Parker J. Palmer, is an eloquent spokesperson for the clearness committee in his books and articles. In *The Courage to Teach* Palmer points out that our current models for engaging one another are so marred by one of a variety of dysfunctional needs—to be nice, to fix things, to give advice—that we actually need new rules to guide our interactions. Palmer writes, "We need ground rules for dialogue that allow us to be present to another person's problems in a quiet, receptive way that encourages the soul to come forth, a way that does not presume to know what is right for the other but allows the other's soul to find its own answers at its own level and pace."[46] The clearness committee provides the model for this kind of dialogue.

As Palmer defines it, the clearness committee is four to six people who meet once for two to three hours at the request of the person desiring "clearness." His outline for what happens in the clearness committee process is both compelling and straightforward. As a seminarian, I was especially taken with Palmer's model as I neared completion of my studies a few years ago. I was like many of my fellow students in that I had worked in one career for several years prior to going to seminary. I was correspondingly not like them in that I chose to attend seminary for avocational reasons. While most of my colleagues anticipated graduation as their segue to a job in pastoral ministry, graduation held no vocational certitude for me. Not knowing what my next step should be, I decided to follow Palmer's clearness committee model as a means of discerning my career path. Based on his writings, the model I followed features seven key elements.

1. *Gather a committee.* The so-called focus person invites four to six persons to be his or her committee.

Following Palmer's admonition to choose diverse individuals, I invited people whom I knew from a variety of contexts. These included three members of the small group I led at church, two chaplains from the hospital where I had completed a chaplaincy internship, a seminary professor, and two seminary friends. Though my committee exceeded by two Palmer's upper limit, it worked very well with eight.

Palmer suggests that one member be appointed "chairperson" to keep the meeting on track and make sure that the rules are followed. Even though I had officially called the meeting, I was grateful to have one of my seminary friends facilitate. Palmer also suggests that one member take notes for the benefit of the focus person's reflections following the meeting. I opted to use a tape recorder so that I could listen to it later as an additional means of discernment. Instead of a note-taker, one person was in charge of making sure the cassette was turned or replaced as needed.

2. *Put it in writing.* The focus person writes a statement about the issue that is circulated to committee members in advance of the meeting. Palmer encourages writing the document in three parts—a clear articulation of the problem, background information, and foreground information (what the focus person sees in the future).

About three weeks prior to the meeting, I submitted three documents to my committee: a two-page summary of the issue that followed Palmer's three-part outline; a two-page statement of my spiritual journey; and a copy of my résumé. Each document represented a significant element for any decisions I might make about a career. Since none of my members had ever served on a clearness committee before, I sent the three documents with a letter that explained what a clearness committee was, how it would operate, and what their responsibilities would be.

3. *Start the meeting.* After opening the meeting with a brief period of silence, the focus person summarizes the nature of the problem.

Prior to beginning the meeting formally, my facilitator first summarized the purpose of the meeting, the rules for the meeting, and answered a few questions. After a brief silence and prayer led by the facilitator, I took about five minutes to restate my concerns about what I should do following seminary. Though I offered no new factual information beyond what the committee had read in the documents, the act of saying it out loud in the presence of people who knew and cared for me was a very reassuring experience. What had become a monumental issue in my own mind was knocked down to size in the act of presenting it within the larger context of the group.

4. *Ask only questions.* During the meeting, committee members give their complete attention to the focus person, but they offer no advice and they engage in no problem solving. What marks this dialogue as distinct is one non-negotiable ground rule: *"Members are forbidden to speak to the focus person in any way except to ask that person an honest, open question."*[47] Palmer points out the rigorous demands of adhering to this rule:

> It means no advice, no overidentification ("I had that problem once, and here is what I did"), no handing off the problem to someone else ("You ought to talk with X about this"), no suggestions of books to read, techniques to use, meditations to practice, therapists to see. Members of the committee may only ask the focus person honest, open questions—questions that do not promote the questioner's agenda but help the focus person discover wisdom within.[48]

Palmer also emphasizes the importance of pacing questions reflectively. The committee must refrain from a "machine-gun" approach and be open to a slower pace that not only allows for periods of silence, but also welcomes them. The focus person, in turn, is encouraged to keep responses relatively brief to allow for still more questions. As Palmer writes, "Some questions seem to require one's whole life story in response; resist the temptation to tell it!"[49] Though committee members are invited to ask all manner of open, honest, and creative questions, it is always the focus person's prerogative to refrain from answering any question. Honoring privacy and vulnerability are central values.

Though they occasionally remarked on how difficult this was in practice, my committee did quite well in adhering to the questions-only rule. They asked what I had liked and disliked about previous jobs, how God had worked in my life in the past, what kind of feelings I had about various vocational options, and what my long-term goals were. Though this went on for almost two hours, several committee members later remarked how quickly the time had passed. None of the questions felt intrusive and so I never felt the need to decline answering. However, in the middle of the process, the facilitator paused the meeting to ask how I was feeling about the proceedings. This gave me an opportunity to affirm that the group was doing exactly what I had hoped, and we continued.

5. *Offer mirroring.* In the last fifteen minutes of the meeting, the facilitator offers the focus person the option of continuing with questions, or moving into a time of feedback from the committee that Palmer calls "mirroring." He writes, "*Mirroring* does not mean an opportunity to give advice. It means reflecting to the focus person things he or she said or did but might not be aware of."[50]

This turned out to be the most helpful part of the process for me. One member noted that though the issue had started out as primarily a vocational concern, the responses I gave seemed to revolve more broadly around my life as a whole. When another member commented that the themes of "spiritual formation" and "communication" were prominent in my responses, three other members immediately affirmed that they had been thinking the same thing. The end result was an understanding on my part that so long as my life as a whole was centered in experiences, people, and events related to either spiritual formation or communication, questions about career would take care of themselves.

6. *Maintain confidentiality.* In addition to the standard rule of confidentiality stipulating that everything that is said

in the meeting remains within the meeting, Palmer cites a second rule for confidentiality: "When the clearness committee is over, members may not approach the focus person with comments or suggestions, for to do so would violate the spirit of the process."[51]

Though I agreed with Palmer's intent, I didn't want my friends to feel like they were now forever prohibited from asking me about my vocational concerns. After the facilitator reiterated the two rules for confidentiality, I assured the committee that while I was not seeking subsequent advice, their ongoing interest in my vocational pursuits was welcomed.

7. *Close the meeting.* In addition to reminding participants about the importance of confidentiality as the meeting draws to a close, Palmer suggests reminding the committee about the meeting's ultimate purpose: "The value of the process is not to be judged by whether the focus person's problem has been 'solved.' Real life does not work that way. This process is about planting seeds . . . and there is no way of knowing when, where, or how those seeds will flower."[52]

I added one element to Palmer's model by deciding to conclude the meeting with communion led by the facilitator. As the ultimate expression of oneness in the Body of Christ, celebration of the Eucharist provided a meaningful way to gather up all that had happened in the meeting and weave it into the fabric of Christian community. The meeting ended not with a focus on me, but with an expression of faith that redirected the group's attention to the source of our *life together* as members of God's family.

Reclaiming Enemy Territory

As the church looks to the future, its vision falls on a spiritual landscape under siege. Reclaiming community through small groups is not an easy solution for relieving the pastoral care demands on overworked clergy, nor is it a thinly veiled therapeutic outlet for the biblically minded. Friend, reclaiming community means nothing less than taking back territory that an enemy has plundered. What makes the battle more insidious still is that the enemy conquers continents of the human heart not through overt aggression, but by slowly turning the soul in small degrees ever inward upon itself. In truth, we are not conquered so much as domesticated into a self-absorbed surrender. "And every state of mind, left to itself," writes C. S. Lewis in *The Great Divorce*, "every shutting up of the creature within the dungeon of its own mind—is, in the end, Hell."[53]

Since I began this chapter with the chilling definition of hell as the "utter loss of community," I will end it with Lewis's distinction of heaven and hell in the *Problem of Pain*:

> We know much more about heaven than hell, for heaven is the home of humanity and therefore contains all that is implied in a glorified human life: but hell was not made for men. It is in no sense *parallel* to heaven: it is "the darkness outside," the outer rim where being fades away into nonentity. . . .
>
> I willingly believe that the damned are, in one sense, successful, rebels to the end; that *the doors of hell are locked on the inside* (emphasis added) . . . they enjoy forever the horrible freedom they have demanded, and are therefore self-enslaved just as the blessed, forever submitting to obedience, become through all eternity more and more free.[54]

If the doors of hell are locked from the inside, then the other side of isolation and despair is *community*, and the key to the unlocking is the spiritual intimacy and formation process afforded by small groups.

CHAPTER FOUR

Team Building Through Spiritual Gifts

Brian K. Bauknight

The gifts [God] gave were . . . to equip the saints for the work of ministry, for building up the body of Christ.
(Ephesians 4:11-12)

Jennifer participated in a "leadership gifts" study with five other young women. Each participant hoped to discover some new direction in her life. Through that study, Jennifer sensed a call to ministry through the local church and clear direction to use her gift of leadership. She relinquished her position as a licensed family therapist with a secular counseling agency. Today she directs a self-supporting counseling service through our church. She is already much sought after and highly regarded by the professional community.

Lisa participated in a four-session spiritual gifts study as part of a different group. Her spiritual gift of "mercy" and her passion for connecting people with meaningful activity were identified and affirmed by the group. The process even-

tually brought her into a new part-time position in the church as outreach coordinator.

These brief examples reveal only a small segment of a twenty-year pilgrimage of team building through spiritual gifts. The experiences of Jennifer and Lisa have been multiplied many times in the ministry and mission of Christ United Methodist Church in suburban Pittsburgh, Pennsylvania.[1]

It is my conviction that leadership in the New Testament church utilized a working ecclesiology of spiritual gifts *(charism)* that inform contemporary ecclesiology and ministry (Ephesians 4:11-12).[2] Paul and others believed that God supplies abundant spiritual gifts to equip the church for "the work of ministry, [and] for building up the body of Christ" (Ephesians 4:12). Evoking one another's spiritual gifts and providing for basic orders of ministry were evident among the earliest communities of believers (Acts 6). Apostles preached the *kerygma* of the risen Christ. Teachers taught people the content and tradition of Christian faith. Elders provided oversight and leadership of the congregation. Administrators handled the business functions of the community. Pastors offered care and counsel to the lonely, the sick, and the bereaved. Deacons served the personal needs of the poor, the widows, and the orphans. Thus the *laos* of God were gifted for ministry (Romans 12:4-8).

How would a commitment to such biblical principles of distributed gifts and shared leadership enable the church to operate? What would a New Millennium of faithful believers look like if an ecclesiology of spiritual gifts described our leadership style? How would such an ecclesiology define (or redefine) the role of clergy and laity in *TheNextChurch*? These and other questions surfaced in my ministry nearly thirty years ago. Through considerable trial and error, through patient learning, through countless occasions of dialogue and refinement, through the discipline of writing and teaching, and through the gracious guidance of our Christlike God, I offer here a functional "doctrine of the church" that defines my pastoral leadership style today, and that may serve as a foundation for mobilizing laity through spiritual gifts.

The Story of Christ United Methodist Church

An open and hospitable community of believers who eagerly invite everyone to connect with God and follow Jesus.[3]

Since 1980 I have served a suburban congregation in the south hills of Pittsburgh, Pennsylvania, currently numbering just more than thirty-two hundred members. I am the third senior minister in the fifty-year history of the congregation. Two ordained elders join me under episcopal appointment on the leadership team. The remaining full-time program staff (including two ordained permanent deacons) all emerged by design out of the congregational membership. Most full-time staff began as part-time lay specialists in a given area and developed with their ministry.

The creative edge in building a leadership team lies within each member of the community of believers. If we are to build a definitive model of the enduring New Testament church, this process will be crucial. Such team building includes paid staffing, lay leadership, and discernment of all spiritual gifts in the body.

Since 1996, we have offered five or six spiritual gift inventory "classes" each year to provide insight and direction regarding places of service and ministry in the church. While not all members choose to participate in these classes, and while we exert no pressure upon persons to do so, the experience leads many members to a fresh understanding of the nature of the church and the promise of more abundant living that has come in Jesus. Many spiritual gifts class "graduates" now serve in areas of leadership and outreach ministries as a result of the process.

My primary vision for the local church is that of a disciple-making community of hospitality. Our vision statement subtitles this section: *We are an open and hospitable community of believers who eagerly invite everyone to connect with God and to follow Jesus.* Forming Christian disciples is our primary task. The operative phrase in the Great Commission is "make disciples" (Matthew 28:19).

My fundamental conviction about church life is this: *There are sufficient spiritual gifts in every community of believers to do what God is calling that community to do in this particular moment of time.* This principle holds true in a church of three thousand members, of three hundred members, or even thirty members. The principle is not my own creation. The precept is taught and modeled in the New Testament—especially in Paul's letter to the Ephesians, which I believe was a circular letter directed to the church as a whole.[4] This understanding can energize and enliven local churches in our time.

Employed Staff

Ever since my local church possessed sufficient financial resources to employ staff, I have believed that such staff should come out of the life of the congregation. This belief had no theological foundation, no ecclesiology at first. I simply employed the principle as a matter of preference. In my first appointment (1964–1971), I instinctively looked to members for part-time positions as secretary and organist. I did not preach or teach on the subject of spiritual gifts during those years. As a matter of fact, I was somewhat confused by the prevailing "charismatic" and "full gospel" movements at the time—both of which provided a fairly narrow definition of spiritual giftedness and a preoccupation with "speaking in tongues."

Then—as now—mainline churches tended *not* to specialize in spiritual gifts. Some church leaders object to the term or fear the reality of distinctly *spiritual* gifts. Some avoid the idea as too complex to implement. Some—including myself at one point—possess little or no information regarding spiritual gifts.

My second appointment (1971–1980) found me serving a rapidly growing suburban community north of Pittsburgh. In this setting, the need and the early promptings for spiritually gifted employed staff began to emerge. One church member already pre-dated me in the office as part-time secretary. Within two years we badly needed an educational assistant with our growing population of younger children. In the providence of God, the right person emerged for us from within the church family at exactly the right time and place. She brought some very specific spiritual gifts to the work, though I could not "name" the specific gifts at the time. However, I knew the gifts were present and appropriately deployed. The barest essentials of a theological and biblical framework began to form.

That moment of finding the right person at the right time, called and gifted for ministry, became a *kairos* moment—a definitive turning point for me in the work of the ministry. A journey began from which I have never turned back. During the nine years in that appointment, we called a youth assistant (who later entered full-time ordained ministry), a financial administrator, a membership care coordinator, a choral director, and several persons in weekday child care and a nursery school—all from within the congregation. Each time we chose to advertise or do an "outside search" for a particular position, the results were less than satisfying. Each time we chose a member, good things happened.

With growing conviction, I patiently and carefully trained the church's personnel committee and others in this methodology of building a staff team. Yet I still did not have a clear biblical understanding of the power and promise of spiritual gifts for all persons. The methodology had no clear, concise theological foundation during those years.

A second—and definitive—turning point came for me at a 1978 continuing education event on "Equipping Laity for Pastoral Ministry" led by Dr. Ronald Sunderland. In the course of three memorable days, I learned (1) the power of spiritual gifts in the New Testament church, (2) the history and cycles of neglect of these gifts over many centuries, and (3) the power of "pastoral care" as one specific lay gift in the authentic Christian community.

I learned that the apostle Paul's way of *doing* church focused on the ecclesiology of spiritual gifts. The Pauline letters provide three separate lists of spiritual gifts apparently in full use in the early church. Paul makes reference to a doctrine of spiritual gifts many times in his letters:

Romans 12:6-8	**1 Corinthians 12; 14:1-12**	**Ephesians 4:7-13**
Prophecy	Healing	Prophets
Ministry	Worker of Miracles	Evangelists
Teaching	Prophecy	Pastors
Exhortation	Discernment of Spirits	Teachers
Generosity	Various Kinds of Tongues	
Leadership	Interpretation of Tongues	
Compassion	Utterance of Wisdom	

These references imply that Paul's readers already had some practical experience organizing the community according to spiritual gifts. Teaching about the Body of Christ and leadership development through spiritual gifts was at work throughout the early church. Yet this principle of spiritual gifts seems to have surrendered to the more dominant hierarchical style of the church leadership by the third and fourth centuries—perhaps even earlier.

In three tightly packed days of study and reflection, Ronald Sunderland taught me more about church history and about myself than I realized. I knew he was right. I knew that my own leadership style as an appointed local church overseer[5] needed to change. I knew there was a power yet to be unlocked in the dynamic design of God for the local church. I knew that I was to move in a new direction from that time forward. I do not suggest that these three days were a "conversion" experience. However, for the first time, the pieces of a puzzle began to fit together. I even found a few previously missing pieces. I discovered why the work of a generalist in ministry was so physically and emotionally draining at times. (I did not have *all* the gifts for ministry.) I discovered why I felt so much more fulfilled in certain parts of my church appointment than others. (I did have *some* of the gifts.) My leadership style would never be the same again. In the closing years of that appointment, and in the nearly two decades of my current appointment, I have worked to perfect and to make this understanding of local church ministry consistent in my calling.

Today I am amazed at the way God works in the church. Through this ancient/modern understanding of the church, many leaders and countless ministries emerge. A woman who has a college degree in chemistry, but who has a deep passion for helping children now serves full time with excellence in children's ministry. A woman who has only a portion of her college work completed serves the church with distinction in areas of Christian formation and adult education. She coordinates a vast and complex program with skill and grace. A man with a college degree in biology serves the church as a gentle, faithful facilities manager. A woman with a college major in industrial engineering does an outstanding job as a director of administration and stewardship. As spiritual gifts surface or become clarified, each team member grows toward a carefully defined staff position, most moving to a full-time basis.[6]

The list goes on. Gifts continue to emerge. The process of incorporating members into staff leadership continues. In recent years we added a full-time chef to the staff team. Lloyd grew up in the church, lived elsewhere for a while, and has now returned to his home church. He has creative gifts and energy for food service that are making a difference in the total ministry of the church. With minimal biblical or theological background, he now understands food service as an important ministry expression in the church. He is ably assisted by a mother-daughter team who have gracious gifts of hospitality and are compensated with a small stipend. Together they make up a gifted leadership team for our "Round Table Ministry."

An urgent need arose for a financial specialist who could step in upon the retirement of our long-tenured director of financial operations. The finance committee requested that we search for a person who was a currently licensed certified public accountant with modern computer skills. Most observers thought we would be unable to find such a person at the salary level we could afford.[7] As we searched the congregation and made the job opening known, a new member emerged who fit the requirements of the job. In our initial interview we were forthright about the salary range. His response: "I am ready to join the ministry team of this church. My wife and I feel that we do not need to earn a large salary in order to be happy or fulfilled at this time in our lives." (His spiritual gift may not be "voluntary poverty," but it might be close!

As chief overseer of the church's life, I provide encouragement toward expression and excellence in spiritual gifts. Such encouragement is my primary role as staff and servant leader. We are members of a leadership team who work in a collegial style. I am the "first among equals" on the team; someone has to be in charge.[8] However, I do not possess many of the gifts that are evident among the staff. In fact, some assumed gifts for the ordained ministry are noticeably absent in me. Therefore, I do not presume to know how they can best do their jobs. I consult regularly, advise when asked, keep the vision of the church before all of us, and pray for each team member. Mostly I expect each staff member to be faithful to the gifts God has given, and to train and enhance those gifts in every way possible.

Expanding the Vision for Spiritual Gifts

Equipping laity for authentic, fulfilling, and God-honoring ministry may be the most important ecclesiological task of our time.

The real work—and the most exciting new dimension—of this ecclesiology is only now developing. What has been true for staffing is also true for the whole body of believers. I remained convinced that every believer has one or more spiritual gifts from God. Every believer finds his or her fulfillment in discovering and using those gifts. All believers have at least one gift. Most have a primary gift *and* two or three secondary gifts.

The role of the pastor in the New Testament is based on spiritual gifts. A pastor in the earliest Christian communities church was a layperson with the God-given facility for listening, caring, and support. Today I am persuaded that healthy and effective local churches are those that take seriously the gift of pastoral care in the life of the congregation. One clear question begs for an answer: What would happen in every local church if lay pastoral gifts were called forth, developed, trained, and utilized on a regular basis? The quantity and quality of congregational care would escalate dramatically. Less burnout would afflict ordained clergy who try to "do it all." Finally, an important biblical principle would be rediscovered: the pastoral ministry of the *laos* of God.

In the early years of my ministry, I personally called out, trained, and supervised persons I believed had the gift of pastoral care. I preached about spiritual gifts using pastoral care as the primary illustration. I discovered an important spiritual truth for my ministry. Not only could some members of the congregation give ongoing care with excellence, but I was set free to be more responsive in other leadership functions and in crisis intervention. Many lay pastors are excellent listeners. They do not have to "solve" the problems of others. They simply provide a Christ-centered caring presence, and—in many instances—a healing presence as well. In infinite Divine wisdom, God has given the church a way to provide quality caring without draining the human energies of one or two individuals.

While early Christian communities provided pastoral care for one another, the exercise of this gift fell dormant quite early in church history. By the third century of the Christian era, the responsibility of pastoral care had fallen into the hands of a few bishops and elders. Perhaps these well-meaning leaders simply assumed power because they felt it was "right." Tragically, the laity let it happen. Martin Luther rediscovered the principle of lay leadership in the sixteenth century with his advocacy for the "priesthood of all believers." John Wesley put the matter into dramatic administrative practice in the eighteenth century with his class leaders. During the circuit rider days of the American frontier, leaders in the small towns came from "class leaders" and pastoral caregivers according to their spiritual gifts. The gifts were called out and lay leaders trained (or coached) by the ordained traveling elders. When the American frontier "settled down," so did the circuit riders. Traveling elders evolved into elders in "station" appointments. The Methodist movement soon became a church led by clergy who were appointed to their "charge." Intentionally or unintentionally, these clergy took over all the leadership of the congregations. An earlier pattern of decline in lay ministry was repeated.[9] *And the laity allowed it to happen!*

Even today United Methodist clergy are asked at ordination if they "will visit from house to house." Ordained clergy make all the hospital calls, visit all the shut-ins, the elderly, and the dying. Clergy do most of the short-term and long-term grief work. All of this is *in addition* to recruiting Sunday school teachers, preaching, teaching classes, training leaders, organizing stewardship drives, doing crisis intervention, participating in community involvement, serving the denomination, and a host of other responsibilities.

Congregations pay their clergy to do the work that belongs by design to *the whole people of God.*

Two matters are now very evident to me for the future church. First, mainliners must release any residual fears we may have regarding supernatural gifts of the Spirit. Second, clergy leaders must willingly let go of church control. God has always had a better plan. In the third millennium of Christendom it is time to renew, refresh, and revitalize the work of spiritual gifts for the whole church.

Gifts for the People of God

Spiritual gifts are allocated by our Creator God. You do not get to "choose" your gifts!

About thirty different spiritual gifts can be clearly discerned in Scripture. Some seem less central in the present day and some gifts are so specialized as to warrant only an appreciative nod. (Examples may include celibacy, voluntary poverty, and martyrdom.) Other gifts are easily subject to misuse and abuse (healing, miracles, and speaking in tongues). While they are biblically authenticated spiritual gifts distributed throughout the Body of Christ, they require a greater openness to the supernatural than some Christians are willing to give. And all the gifts identified in the New Testament require complex interpretation to bring them from the first-century biblical context into the twenty-first century.

According to the Willow Creek model, approximately two dozen gifts remain highly visible and appropriate in the life of today's believing community.[10] How shall we discover, discern, and name these gifts in a believer? One solution is to make such discernment the task of the clergy. Appointed or called clergy leaders *could* argue they are the primary discerners of spiritual gifts. However, I find this somewhat dangerous, if not arrogant. Not all clergy have equal facility for distinguishing or discriminating among either the gifts or the persons so endowed. I prefer to think of the clergy leaders as the vision-planters regarding spiritual gifts in congregational life. Ordained clergy are not the sole proprietors or authenticators of God's gracious offering in spiritual gift ecclessiology.

Another possibility (especially in the larger multiple staff church) is to make gift discernment the work of the staff leadership team. Each member of the team has a calling to watch over a segment of the congregation, notice emerging gifts, and respond to those gifts in leadership development on behalf of the whole church. I ask every staff member on my team to have some responsibility in this regard. The matter is written into each position description. The process often works well. However, once again the method may limit or minimize the possibilities of God's work in a particular church.

A third possibility opens the matter up to the whole congregation. For example, when preparing to call and train a new group of lay pastors, we might make this statement to the congregation: "Whom do you know in this community of believers who has a gift for listening and caring? Whom might you seek out if you needed a good listening ear? Write down the name or names on a piece of paper and hand them to one of the ordained clergy." Those whose names appear multiple times on such lists have a strong probability for possessing the gift of pastoral care.

At Christ Church we try to combine these last two possibilities as a kind of hybrid for the authentication of individual gifts by the entire congregation, initiated by staff discernment. For example, when we are seeking the best possible teachers of children in the Sunday school, we place an insert in the worship guide: "Whom would you most like to teach your child in the Sunday school next year? Who, in your experience, has the gift of teaching? Place the name or names on the insert this morning for further consideration." In each instance we might get a dozen or more names. The spiritual leadership team, comprised of lay and clergy leaders, pays careful attention to those names that appear more than once in the responses. A list of candidates emerges— those who may be invited to enter a period of training and personal assessment. The nomination process is human and thus never perfect. But the procedure *does surface many good names.* Frequently, the names are persons we had never considered previously. God opens up new gifts and new servants in the Kingdom work. The people of God are constantly at work in the discernment process. The final decision to assign ministry tasks rests with the leadership team.

A Total Church Plan

God provides the right person with the right gifts at the right time!

For the past several years we have inaugurated and utilized an intentional plan for discerning spiritual gifts in the life of the community. We now employ a spiritual gift inventory to assist people in finding their place in God's work. A growing number of such inventories are available today. Some are very simple and direct. Others are more complex and time consuming. We have settled upon a four-session class using the Network material from the Willow Creek Community Church in South Barrington, Illinois. Willow Creek remains in the forefront among teaching churches on this and other issues related to mobilizing laity. Furthermore, they allow maximum flexibility in the use of their material once you have purchased it. (For more information or a catalogue, write to Willow Creek Resources, Willow Creek Association, P.O. Box 3188, Barrington, IL 60011-3188, or call 708-765-0070. The student's book *[Participant's Guide]* is available through Zondervan Press in most large religious bookstores. A starter kit is available for close examination.)

We have not fully examined other spiritual gift inventories. I have looked briefly at two much simpler inventories (one of which takes only about an hour), and have declined to use them because they are "too simple." We have elected to make the Spiritual Gift Inventory a substantive educational and Christian formation experience, not a quick test or "fast" spiritual food.

We utilize a humorous and helpful video introduction from Willow Creek senior minister, Bill Hybels. We also purchased the overhead graphics and summaries as a teaching tool. We ask each participant to purchase a student book. What was initially designed as an eight-week class, we have reduced to four weekday afternoons or evenings, or a Wednesday evening, Friday evening, and Saturday morning time frame. We also incorporate a class (mostly younger mothers) into seventy-five minutes each on four consecutive Wednesday afternoons while children are in choir rehearsals. Suburban lifestyles and schedules require offering any series of short-term classes in a flexible format. We believe the classes are important enough to make as many options available as possible. Our only requirement is that persons be present for each session in the series. The training is an unfolding process and requires a clear progression through the material.

Persons are usually invited to participate in the class in one of three ways: (1) an open invitation to everyone in the congregation, (2) a verbal invitation to all new members at each final new-member orientation class held about five times a year, or (3) a personal letter of invitation from me to the newest members, to recent *Disciple Bible Study*[11] graduates, and to other selected groups as appropriate. In addition, various staff members will offer a personal word of encouragement to particular persons with whom they work. Classes average from ten to twenty-five persons in each series—with twenty to twenty-five being the optimum size for good discussion and interaction. The newest members of the congregation generally make up the largest percentage of participants. Long-standing members seem to feel less inclined or less needful for such training. Each class has several participants who are not (yet) members. A few from other churches join us because they have heard about the sessions and want to participate.

The **first session** includes the video and overview of what we hope to accomplish. We then launch into what is acknowledged to be the most difficult part of the inventory. *What is your passion?* What do you really like to do? What topic or activity could keep you talking late into the night? Some participants quickly name a passion. Perhaps it is children, or family, or special need adults. Perhaps it is music or hosting events in the home. Some persons are puzzled by this initial question. If their passion is woodworking or sailing or walking or reading (to name only a few), they see no connection between this reality and their spiritual gifts. We counsel patience and trust in the process. We counsel prayerful  preparation for the assessment—a quiet time alone at home for reflection and discernment. Participants are asked to list two or three passions in their lives, and then to rank them in order. They are asked to return to the next session prepared to share with their small group the discovery process of their primary passion in a smaller group.

In the **second session,** participants spend considerable time debriefing their struggle with the issue of passion. Everyone is encouraged to name at least one passion regardless of how difficult such naming may seem. Class facilitators then introduce the New Testament teaching about history and theology of spiritual gifts: *"To each is given* the manifestation of the Spirit for the common good" (1 Corinthians 12:7, emphasis mine). No one is left out. No one is left off the gift list. To deny that you have one or more spiritual gifts is to deny part of the creative work of God in the world. Gifts have no automatic ties to your educational or socioeconomic level or profession. Gifts are not limited by race, ethnic background, gender, or sexual orientation. For example, as a professional clergyperson, my own primary gift is that of administration. Secondary gifts are encouragement and giving. Leadership—which I *wanted* to be my number one gift—is fourth.

Gifts are given to be used in the work of the ministry of the church. "Since you are eager for spiritual gifts, strive to excel in them for building up the church" (1 Corinthians 14:12). Spiritual gifts differ from talents. You may be born with a talent for music or intellectual pursuits or artistic expression. However, a talent is not a spiritual gift *unless or until* it is used "for the work of ministry, for building up the body of Christ" (Ephesians 4:12). Peter reminds his readers (certainly in the spirit of Paul) that gifts are not to be wasted or put on a shelf, but used: "Serve one another with whatever gift each of you has received." (1 Peter 4:10).

In the mainline denominations, people tend not to believe that they have spiritual gifts to share. Of those who believe, few declare that they are actually utilizing their gifts in any clear or faithful fashion. Scripture reminds us that while we have gifts that differ (Romans 12:6), we *all* have gifts and the gifts we individually have been given are for the common good. This biblical background consumes a large part of session two.

Participants are then given the Willow Creek Network spiritual gift inventory to complete at home. Again, we counsel prayer before beginning the inventory: "Let the will and love of God flow through your responses." Included with the personal inventory is the strong suggestion for three "observation assessments" by others who know you well. They may be a spouse, a son or daughter, an extended family member, a close friend, or a work colleague. Others may see gifts in you that you may not see in yourself. Others may also confirm what you see in yourself. Three observation assessment forms are provided to each class member. A system of scoring and compiling the answers is explained. The purpose of this exercise is to discover your primary and secondary spiritual gift(s) as God's blessing in your Christian life.

Excitement is usually high when participants return for the **third session**. Some are pleased. Some are amazed. Some are dumbfounded. "I never thought I had the gift of leadership . . . creative communication . . . giving . . . evangelism . . . pastoral care." Together in small groups, members share the discoveries and insights gained from the personal inventory and the observations by others. As a total group, we list the primary gifts believed to be present in the room. Often we find large clusters of similar gifts within the group. Sometimes, the list is long—we don't limit spiritual gifts to just those listed in the New Testament. We have even dared to add to the biblical list current manifestations of giftedness in believers.

I say to every new-member class in the church: "I have no idea what gifts are emerging in this group of persons who are about to unite with this church. I look forward to the unfolding of your gifts in the ministry of this congregation over the next few years." The spiritual gifts classes validate that expectation and reward the enthusiasm of those words.

The **fourth and final session** deals with personal style. How are you wired and organized? Are you more spontaneous or more structured? And how are you energized? By people or by tasks? In what ways will you be more comfortable in using your spiritual gifts and passions? The simple inventory for this final segment is a modified version of the Meyers-Briggs Type Indicator with which many readers will be familiar.[12]

Not all of us are comfortable with unstructured settings. Not all persons are organized around structure or energized by other people. For example, I am a person who thrives on *tasks* that motivate and encourage people. However, any informal gathering in a room with a lot of *people* whom I do not know well is sometimes exhausting for me. I do not naturally remember names well. I know others who are highly energized by meeting new people. They not only remember names, but also remember details that will connect these people with others. The more people they meet, the higher their energy level becomes. I experience the opposite. We are created differently in our personal style, just as we have differing spiritual gifts.

The closing session of the class receives responses to the personal style inventory. We suggest that most believers will find their deepest fulfillment in the center of the "bull's-eye" of **passion, personal style, and spiritual gift**.

In summarizing all four sessions, we try to reinforce the follow points:

• Spiritual gifts are for a lifetime, not just a season.

• People who go with the flow of their spiritual gifts very seldom burn out.

• Spiritual gifts are for the whole work of the ministry (including outreach to the community and the world) and for the building up of the Body of Christ (congregational care and nurture).

• Servant leadership is the most appropriate style for utilizing spiritual gifts.

• Each of us should work with the results of the inventory until we have found a place of fulfillment and service, and know the truest peace of God in our lives.

Upon completion of the series (and before leaving the final session), we "require" a one-hour follow-up consultation for each participant with a trained lay consultant.[13] Those who forget or who are not sure of their schedule are carefully and systematically pursued until they commit to a time and place. They meet to discuss the results of their learnings in the class. Suggestions are made regarding possible places of service, inside and outside the congregation: a Sunday school assistant or food bank worker; a choir member or community tutor; a ministry team member or ministry team chair; a hospitality greeter or homeless ministry worker.

Wherever appropriate, the consultation report is shared

with a clergy or lay staff member for further contact, invitation, or training. *Someone* always follows up on the completed report to help facilitate members serving in their motivated area of giftedness.

The Church as Deployment Center

The Church Is God's Best Hope for a Sane and Stable World

Over a period of three years, approximately two hundred congregational members and friends completed the spiritual gifts assessment process—a little less than 10 percent of the active membership of Christ United Methodist Church. We continue to offer the classes quarterly and the results are apparent. People who love people work with people—often openly and publicly. People who love tasks perform tasks—often quietly behind the scenes. New teachers have emerged for adult education. New lay pastors are providing care and a listening presence with the convalescing, the elderly, the shut-ins, and the dying. New names surface for the administrative tasks. New persons with a heart of compassion for the lonely and the outcast now find a way to joyfully serve. New households and individuals with the distinctly spiritual "gift of giving" are providing strong financial support for the total ministry.

All of the assessment data is entered into our computerized membership data bank for use as needed. We can key in a name and view the individual or family profile brought up on the computer screen. We can scan to see if that person has participated in the spiritual gifts inventory class, or completed their personal consultation. Another keystroke brings up the results of the assessment for review and possible follow-up. The goal is to be able to connect gift resources with human need in a high-tech, high-touch way.

Every member who has been through the training has a profile in the computer system: his or her passion, three primary spiritual gifts, and personal style. I have used this new membership data bank several times to positive and productive advantage. Other members of the spiritual leadership team use the data bank with far greater frequency. The church nominating process is simplified and given a theological foundation of spiritual giftedness.

In many ways, we are only in the beginning stages of combining an ancient Christian truth (spiritual gifts) with new technology (computer data bases). As with any other Christian resource, the methodology must be used regularly and faithfully. Old habits of "selecting" leaders need to die so that a new process may be born. We all need periodic reminders as to both the discipline and the foundation undergirding spiritual gifts in the church. Such gentle but constant reminders are regularly incorporated into the pulpit ministry, the educational ministry, the newsletter, and the organizational principles of the church.

I believe we are on the leading edge of the way in which faithful congregations will do ministry in the future. We are moving, I trust, toward a more faithful way of following Jesus. Again, *I believe there are sufficient spiritual gifts in every church to do what God is calling that church to do in this particular moment of time.* I commend the process of discovering, evoking, and naming spiritual gifts in mobilizing laity for the work of the ministry. As one who deeply loves the local church, and as one who has been privileged to learn and grow in over thirty-five years of servant leadership, I can assure you that it will transform your ecclesiology and potential for equipping the saints in the electronic age.

CHAPTER FIVE

The Seeker Service in the Mainline Church

Eric Park

The gospel of Jesus Christ has gone forth in every era with power to convert human hearts. . . . Our task as Christ's disciples is to embody and articulate the never-changing good news of available salvation in a manner that the emerging generation can understand.[1]

"What have I gotten myself into," I thought to myself as I stood on the newly created platform in the sanctuary. It was the first Sunday night in February of 1996, and my task was to greet the congregation at the first *seeker-sensitive worship* service at Christ United Methodist Church.[2] Three hundred fifty people, many of whom were there simply to satisfy their curiosity, had gathered to experience the experimental worship event.

The theater lights, purchased to create some spectacle around the service, were nearly blinding, so much so that I could barely see the congregation. Large speakers, monitors, and cables surrounded the platform, tangible reminders that this technological worship event represented an intersection

121

between ancient and future church. The screen behind me and the video projector in the balcony signaled to the congregation that the hymnals in the pew racks would not be required during this occasion of worship. Theater props were in place in the upper altar area for that evening's dramatic vignette. The band members were also in place, positioned around the raised platform with their instruments plugged in. And there I stood in jeans and a polo shirt.

As one who loves religious history and tradition, I could not help comparing my journey into seeker-sensitive worship with that of another reluctant iconoclast: John Wesley. The Anglican priest, out of whose thinking and vision the Methodist movement emerged in the mid-eighteenth century, was compelled to take his preaching outside the walls of Anglican architecture and into the open fields. By doing so, he enabled the gospel of Jesus Christ to intersect the lives of common men and women who would never find their way into the ornateness of a sanctuary. Wesley describes his transition to "open air" preaching in this fashion:

> Being thus excluded from the churches, and not daring to be silent, it remained only to preach in the open air; which I did at first, not out of choice, but necessity; but I have since seen abundant reason to adore the wise providence of God herein, making a way for myriads of people, who never troubled any church, nor were likely to do so, to hear that word which they soon found to be the power of God unto salvation.[3]

As a United Methodist, I am particularly proud of Wesley's boldness in this regard, a holy zeal that inspired him, and others like him, to seek out new ways in which to articulate the *kergyma* and to be the church. Woven into the very fabric of my denominational heritage is a stubborn refusal to permit the church to wallow in the stagnant waters of irrelevancy.[4]

I believe many modern experiments in seeker-sensitive worship (sometimes called contemporary or alternative worship) are current manifestations of that same holy zeal that inspired innovators like John and Charles Wesley. If so, then seeker-sensitive worship can never be rightly described as something outside the parameters of the mainline Christian tradition, as though it were somehow an ecclesical oddity without precedent. On the contrary, seeker-sensitive worship takes its cue from Wesley's open-air preaching, Luther's and Calvin's passion for reformation, even the apostle Paul's willingness to "become all things to all people, that [he] might by all means save some" (1 Corinthians 9:22).

As I stood there prepared to greet the congregation, I realized that I was entering into a different kind of open-air preaching—a kind of preaching in which the "open air" was not a grassy field but rather the postmodern ethos where a new generation can be engaged.[5] In Wesley's open-air services, the listeners were the outcasts that the church had rejected. In my "open-air" services, the listeners are the spiritual seekers that the church has ignored.

Seeker-sensitive worship at its worst can be a futile effort to entertain nominal believers with hollow spectacle and truncated proclamation. At its best, however, seeker-sensitive worship is the most recent incarnation of the church's desire to find its voice admist cultural transitions and paradigm shifts. When actualized with integrity, seeker-sensitive worship becomes an effective means to incorporate a new language to tell an old story, thereby reaching the unchurched generations, which Wesley described as the "myriads of people, who never troubled any church, nor [are] likely to do so."[6]

A Personal Journey

My passion for seeker-sensitive worship is preceded by a love for traditional liturgy. I am a child of the church, the son of a pastor, reared in a milieu of spirited hymn-singing and colorful vestments. The Lord's Prayer, the Apostles' Creed, and the Gloria Patri were a second language to me.

During my college years, I sang in a chamber choir that regularly provided music for the Sunday morning Roman Catholic campus mass. My participation in the Roman liturgy only intensified my appreciation of more ancient expressions for Christian worship. After college, I attended a mainline seminary in which my weekly worship took place in a Gothic cathedral, complete with chimes and incense ("smells and bells," according to Protestant vernacular). I came out of theological school very much a purist in matters of worship. "It is not worship's job to be relevant, it is worship's job to be faithful," I had convinced myself.

There was absolutely nothing in my church background or seminary experience that would bring about in me any recognition of the merits of contemporary seeker-sensitive worship. What began to transform my thinking, however, were conversations I had with unchurched friends and acquaintances—men and women who were neither atheistic nor agnostic, but honest seekers desiring access to the life of the church.

My friend Lou, for example, is the proprietor of my favorite comic book store. (My fascination with comic books is fodder for another venue!) Early in our friendship, Lou asked me the question that always evokes at least a split-second of anxiety in the hearts and minds of clergy: "What do you do for a living?"

"Well, Lou, I'm a United Methodist pastor."

"Does that mean you preach?" he asked.

"Yeah, I do my best."

He smiled. "You're a preacher who reads comic books?"

"What's your point, Lou?"

"Nothing," he said. "I guess it's just that I always thought you church folks only read boring stuff."

"Like what?" I inquired.

"Like the Bible," he responded, realizing immediately that he had said something he probably shouldn't have.

"Do you honestly believe that, Lou? Do you honestly believe that the Bible is nothing more than boring literature?"

His response was significant. "No," he answered, "I guess

the Bible itself isn't so boring. But you church folks seem to do everything you can to make it boring."

"What do you mean by that?"

"Well," he said, "believe it or not, I've been to six or seven different Protestant churches in the last three years, because I really would like to find a good church for my family and me. But every church I've visited has been about the same. People singing music that doesn't sound anything at all like the music I listen to. People reading prayers that don't sound anything at all like the kind of prayers that I make when I do try to pray. Preachers preaching sermons that sound good, but that don't have anything to do with the real world."

He paused, as though he were reluctant to share his next thought. "It's frustrating," he admitted, "because I left those church services feeling like I had just watched a play in a foreign language and missed the point."

His words brought about twenty seconds of silence as thick as it was awkward. "Lou," I finally said, "how can the church do better in this regard?"

"I don't know," he answered. "It's your job to figure that out! All I know is that I need a church that speaks a language I can understand. A church that tells me that God is real and that God has something to do with my little corner of the world."

That conversation was pivotal for me. I left the comic book store with both a deeper sensitivity to the journey of a genuine seeker, and a holy desire to bring about seeker-sensitive worship in my church setting. In short, the voice of Christ behind the words of Lou was calling me to prepare myself for new directions and dynamic changes in my church.

What Exactly Is a Seeker?

We suffer from a poverty of nomenclature when speaking of the "unchurched." Any vocabulary we use runs the risk of sounding trite or worse, condescending. Could it not be argued that all of us are "seekers"—troubled souls or restless hearts seeking to know the One who breathed into us the breath of life, longing to be authentically human and meaningfully connected to the Source?

Despite the limitations of language, I am willing to accept the label "seeker" as at least partially descriptive of persons like Lou. A seeker, according to my definition, is a person of any age, although primarily between twenty to forty-five (since that is the age group most conspicuously absent from our church pews), who seeks *personal transformation, spiritual wholeness, and community connectedness,* but cannot find these aspects in the context of what the church has traditionally offered on Sunday mornings. "Keep in mind," writes Lee Strobel, "there are at least fifty-five million unchurched adults in the country. Think how many might return to the church if it were only more sensitive to their needs and relevant to their lives."[7]

A seeker, in other words, is a restless soul yearning for truth communicated in an understandable language, and love embodied in a relevant community of faith.[8]

Seekers Among the Boomer and X Generations

It is worth noting that, perhaps only fifty years ago, as many as 85 to 95 percent of the adults in our country were exposed to some kind of Christian education.[9] The majority of Americans held membership in a local church, even if this membership was not a particularly serious religious connection, or at least attended services on Christmas and Easter. There was, in most families, at least a modicum of familiarity with the Christian narrative.

In this predominantly churched cultural setting, the typical pattern was this: In their late teens or early twenties, people would drift away from the local church, partly because of time constraints, partly because of indifference. Then, after a few years, when marriage and parenthood had softened their hearts to life's deeper realities, these same people would reenter the life of the church, along with their families, no doubt in an effort to ground themselves in something more profound than their careers and social network. For decades, this cultural-ecclesial pattern could be relied upon. Churches would bid farewell to their high school graduates and college students, knowing that there was a good chance of their eventual return as young adults. "Train up a child . . ." was a general proverb often claimed as an absolute promise.

Times have changed, and the breakers of this pattern were the baby boomers (people born after World War II, from 1946 to 1960). The Boomers did indeed leave the church in their late teens and early twenties, following the predictable cultural pattern. However, as a generation, they did not return.[10] Even after marriage and parenthood, the Boomers never fully reentered the life of the local church. As a result, many Boomers (and their children, Generation X) possess what George Hunter describes as "little or no Christian memory, background, or vocabulary."[11]

There are significant sociological reasons for the Boomers' pattern-breaking behavior, not the least of which is the proclivity to individualism that has undergirded much of America's cultural development in the last several decades.[12] The Boomers were raised in a milieu characterized by grandiose notions of self-sufficiency and self-reliance. It is difficult for the church to find a place for such a worldview.

Many are the ramifications of the Boomers' ecclesial departure, but none is more important than this: Because of their lack of church connectedness, many Boomers have chosen to raise their children entirely outside the community of faith. As a result, there are millions of young Americans in their twenties and thirties who, apart from the occasional wedding or funeral, have never even set foot inside a local church.

127

It is common among the Boomers and GenXers to find those who have never heard of the Lord's Prayer, much less the Apostles' Creed. They are certainly not familiar with the content of John 3:16 or the Twenty-third Psalm. "Amazing Grace" and "How Great Thou Art" are not on their list of favorite tunes. Organ music is as foreign to them as the vestments worn by the clergy. The reality of the postmodern world is there is a burgeoning population of people who do not speak the language of traditional Christianity. Nor do they desire to learn that language. Why should they? Traditional church, after all, has precious little, if anything, to do with their life experience.

And yet, in spite of their lack of interest in traditional worship, perhaps somewhere in the deepest chambers of their souls, this present, unchurched generation of biblical and ecclesiastical illiterates long to hear the good news in terms of their own language and culture.

Biblical Imperatives

As the church of Jesus Christ, our ministry is not built upon the shifting sands of contemporary philosophy. Rather, our ministry is built upon the time-tested solid rock of biblical truth. Therefore, it is imperative for the church to explore the question of whether or not there are impulses present in Scripture that would lead us to be open to the possibility of seeker-sensitive worship. Once my eyes were opened to the need for seeker worship through the operation of God's Spirit through encounter with Lou and other seekers, I went back to Scripture and found clear support for an ecclesiology of seeker worship.

At the beginning of my present appointment, one of my first assignments was to meet weekly with a ten-member seeker task force. Our mission was to create and implement a Sunday night contemporary worship service that might provide an Orthodox (= right worship) environment in which a seeker might be led to experience the reality of Christ. At the end of one of those early task force meetings, I invited the ten members to spend the next week pouring themselves into Scripture, searching prayerfully for any biblical impulse that might support our task.

A week later, the task force met again, and it quickly became clear to me they had done their homework. One man (Grant) made reference to Jesus' words in the Great Commission: "Go therefore and make disciples of all nations" (Matthew 28:19).

"Those words of Scripture have been very much on my heart this week," Grant said. "I hear in those words a biblical call to find creative new ways to bring the gospel to those people who aren't sitting in the church pews on Sunday morning. Isn't that what we're all about with this task force?"

A woman on the task force (Judith) shared with the group that she was particularly drawn to the apostle Paul's call to cultural relevance in the Corinthian correspondence: "I have become all things to all people, that I might by all means save some" (1 Corinthians 9:22).

"I don't think Paul is telling us to compromise our faith in this scripture," Judith said. "But I do believe that Paul is telling us that it is appropriate, even necessary, to change our style and our method in order to communicate the gospel more effectively to the people around us. That's what I think we're doing with this new contemporary worship service. We're 'becoming all things to all people' for the sake of Christ."

"All I have to do is look at the last psalm in the psalter," another woman (Miriam) reported.

> Praise him with trumpet sound;
>> praise him with lute and harp!
> Praise him with tambourine and dance;
>> praise him with strings and pipe!

129

Praise him with clanging cymbals;
praise him with loud clashing cymbals!
Let everything that breathes praise the LORD!
Praise the LORD! (Psalm 150:3-6)

"If that isn't a biblical call to celebrate creative and contemporary worship," Miriam said, "I don't know what is."

Still another task force member (Robin) said that she was struck by the number of "seekers" encountered by Jesus in the unfolding of his ministry: Nathanael, coming to Jesus on Philip's invitation simply to find out what Jesus was all about; the Samaritan woman at the well, eagerly questioning Jesus about the living water he came to provide; blind Bartimaeus, calling out to Jesus from the roadside, desperate for the healing touch that Jesus might offer; the lone woman with an expensive jar of perfume; and Zacchaeus, the "wee little man" climbing the tree simply to catch a glimpse of the wonderworker from Nazareth.

"What amazes me," said Robin, "is the way in which Jesus went out of his way to embrace these seekers, even going so far as to break some cultural taboos for the sake of helping them. If Jesus was willing to go that far for seekers in his time, shouldn't we be willing to at least create a worship service for the seekers in our time?"

This was one of the most meaningful discussions I have ever participated in as a pastor. By the end, I had a much greater appreciation of the spiritual depth of our seeker task force. Furthermore, I had a much clearer understanding of the primary motivation behind what we were doing. By creating a contemporary worship service, we were not simply jumping on a relevant bandwagon or trying the newest gimmick. Rather, we were interpreting the biblical impulse present throughout Scripture in light of our current encounters with seekers in our midst.

A Typical Seeker-Sensitive Service at Christ United Methodist Church

After months of prayerful planning, the seeker task force settled on an order of worship for our Sunday night seeker-sensitive worship event. Although there is always the freedom to alter the format whenever there is a need to do so, this original order of worship has served as our liturgical roadmap for the last four years. I share it now in the hope that it will provide a clearer understanding of how seeker-sensitive worship unfolds in the context of my ecclesial setting. The liturgically oriented reader may notice intentional parallels to traditional worship, but the structure and flow of the service has the effect of freedom and spontaneity as well as rhyme and reason.

- Music from The SUNDAY NIGHT Band (a ten-minute period of praise music as the congregation gathers; the sanctuary lights are up, but dimmed, so that curious seekers will not be intimidated by what I call an "institutional brightness")
- Greeting and Brief Announcement Period—done by the pastor
- Drama illustrating/embodying the theme of the service
- Music from The SUNDAY NIGHT Band (normally an up-tempo song that celebrates the goodness and grace of God)
- A Time of Chorus Singing led by the band (We normally sing four or five choruses during this segment, making sure that at least one chorus is confessional in nature. There was consensus among the members of our seeker task force that the discipline of confession should be woven into the very fabric of the SUNDAY NIGHT liturgy.)
- Evening Prayer (Initiated by a worship leader, this is a time of intercessory prayer that brings before God the

131

needs of the world and community. The worship leader occasionally will invite the congregation into a time of silent confession of sin, culminating in the corporate singing of "The Lord's Prayer.")

- Explanation of the Evening Offering done by the worship leader
- Instrumental Music from The SUNDAY NIGHT Band (as the offering is received)
- Chorus: "Open Our Eyes, Lord" (sung each week before the reading of Scripture)
- Scripture announced and read by the pastor
- Message offered by the pastor
- From The SUNDAY NIGHT Band (normally a more meditative song that helps to illuminate the content of the message)
- Closing Prayer offered by the pastor
- Chorus: "Lord, Be Glorified" (sung each week at the conclusion of the service)

It is worth noting that we do offer a ministry to children as part of SUNDAY NIGHT, including a nursery for infants and "J.A.M." (Jesus And Me) sessions for elementary-aged children. Also, a well-organized team of ushers and greeters makes sure the ministry of hospitality is present each week.

The Nonnegotiables of SUNDAY NIGHT

Another vitally important component of those early seeker task force meetings was our discussion of what we have come to describe as the "nonnegotiables." These are the pillars of our Sunday night service that keep us accountable to our original vision and help us to honor both the identity and integrity of Christian worship. Since we refer to our contemporary service simply as "SUNDAY NIGHT," it made good sense for us to use "S-U-N-D-A-Y-N-I-G-H-T" as the acronym for identifying our nonnegotiables.

Nonnegotiable Number 1: Sermons That Are Solidly Biblical, Engagingly Conversational, and Unapologetically Relevant

I was trained to be a preacher in the classical Protestant tradition. Since Scripture is primary, you begin with the biblical text. Spend the better part of the sermon helping the congregation to understand the historical context out of which the text emerged. Then, if there is any time left, articulate one or two applications of the text in order to make it practical.

In order to engage the sometimes skeptical mind and heart of the genuine seeker, however, a much more topical approach to preaching is required. Instead of beginning with a biblical text and moving eventually (perhaps) to a topic, the sermonic presentation in a seeker-sensitive service normally reverses that order. At our contemporary service, for example, I usually begin the sermon by introducing a topic (marriage, divorce, anger, joy, priorities, violence, love, sin, forgiveness). When the topic has been sufficiently clarified, I carry that topic into the biblical narrative, so that the topic itself might be weighed, judged, illuminated, and finally redeemed by the transforming truth of Scripture.

Some would argue that topical preaching is an inferior homiletical approach, that it makes Scripture into little more than a contemporary self-help book. I disagree. After preaching for nearly four years at our contemporary service, I have come to discover that topical preaching can protect the integrity of Scripture as effectively as any other homiletical style. I believe, in fact, that topical preaching, because of its commitment to relevance, is perhaps the best means we have by which to enable a seeker to hear the Word of God in a way that is authentic.

Nonnegotiable Number 2: Unwavering Commitment to Excellence in All Areas of Worship

We have all sat through some screechy solos during worship! During such an awkward experience, the spiritually mature worshiper might be able to say something like this: "Wow! That is painful to the ear! But I know that that person is doing his or her best, and so I will endeavor to worship God in the midst of it." The seeker, on the other hand, who might have nothing at all invested in the church, will not hesitate to "bail out" of a worship service if there is a consistent rendering of awkward mediocrity. "If that's all the effort they are going to put into this," the seeker might say, "then it isn't worth my time."

Therefore, any church interested in creating a seeker-sensitive worship service had best commit to excellence in all areas of worship: music, drama, preaching, sound and lighting, hospitality. I emphasize the significance of this commitment because, practically speaking, excellence honors the seeker. More important, from a theological perspective, excellence honors God.

Nonnegotiable Number 3: Nuanced Explanation and Interpretation of the Weekly Offering

A vital component of Christian worship is the opportunity to bring to God a portion of our financial resources, that God might be glorified by the offering of our best gifts. The seeker, however, often carries into worship a suspicion that the church teeters on the brink of being a money-hungry institution. "I knew it," a seeker might be inclined to say at offering time. "This church is only after my wallet."

At SUNDAY NIGHT, we endeavor to explain and interpret the offering for the congregation each week. We make clear, for example, that no offering is expected from first-time visitors, since they may not be prepared to give. But for the benefit of people who have made SUNDAY NIGHT their primary service of worship, we articulate each week that the offering is not merely a thoughtless financial transaction. Rather, it is a sacred moment of worship in which we have the opportunity to honor God with the boldness and faithfulness of our giving.

Nonnegotiable Number 4: Dramatic Vignettes That Highlight Issues Surrounding the Weekly Theme

Over the last three years, we have developed a drama team, the responsibility of which is to offer a weekly vignette at SUNDAY NIGHT. We began this team with one director and six actors. We now have six directors and well over twenty actors. Their ministry, greatly cherished by the SUNDAY NIGHT congregation, has become one of the most meaningful and celebrated features of our service.

For our dramatic material, we most often use the Willow Creek dramas (available through Zondervan publishing). I find them to be well written and not at all heavy-handed in their dramatic approach.

It was tempting at first to settle for a monthly drama instead of a weekly drama. It took a lot of extra effort and commitment to offer this feature weekly, but was well worth it.

Nonnegotiable Number 5: Advertising That Is Bold and Innovative

When our seeker task force turned its attention to the issue of publicity, there was consensus that we did not want our advertising to be arrogant and self-serving. At the same time, we agreed that it was important for us to make known to our community the fact that our contemporary service existed, especially since it was fairly unique to the south hills of Pittsburgh.

We began with newspaper articles and advertisements, followed by several months of radio commercials. This early publicity emphasized the point that SUNDAY NIGHT incorporated a new worship language that might be heard meaningfully by those who are spiritually hungering for a contemporary expression of praise.

In our boldest advertising endeavor, we established a relationship with a local movie theater, the management of which agreed to include a slide for SUNDAY NIGHT in the rotation of slides that appeared before each movie. This type of target advertising, though highly expensive, is well worth it if it means communicating the nature of our ministry directly to those we are attempting to reach.

Nonnegotiable Number 6: Yielding to Meaningful Evaluation and Criticism

Our SUNDAY NIGHT worship team meets monthly to celebrate our contemporary service and hold it in prayer. Another important part of those monthly meetings is making time to critique the service and share criticisms we have received from the congregation. Such criticism, although not always easy to hear, helps us make a good worship service even better.

Nonnegotiable Number 7: New Musical Language—Contemporary Christian Music That Is Stylistically Appropriate for the Sunday Night Congregation

Nonnegotiable Number 8: Instrumental Innovation—Keyboards, Synthesizers, Guitars, and Percussion

With all due respect to the importance of preaching, music is to SUNDAY NIGHT what breathing is to the human body: life, vitality, centeredness. Every local church interested in doing contemporary worship must first determine what contemporary musical style it wants to embrace: jazz, pop, classic rock, R&B, folk. But no matter what musical style a church chooses to incorporate, one thing is for certain: It must be of good quality, and it must be consistently pleasing.

When I began thinking about the music ministry for SUNDAY NIGHT, I had the proverbial "ace in the hole" in the person of my wife, Tara. She is what I like to call a franchise player, the unique talent around which a team can be built. As gifted a pianist as she is a vocalist, I knew that Tara was excited to be a vital part of SUNDAY

NIGHT's music ministry. After a month of research, phone calls, and face-to-face conversations, I had assembled a volunteer band around Tara that included a keyboardist, a bass guitarist, and a drummer, all of whom had musical gifts and passions that were beyond my greatest expectations. Along the way, we added an exceptional guitarist. Our music team was complete.

Much to my amazement and delight, our band members have taken their music ministry beyond the walls of our church, playing regularly at local coffeehouses and concert events. In addition, the band is in the process of completing its second CD of original music. Influenced by the "arena rock" of secular groups from the 1970s (Kansas, Styx, and Fleetwood Mac, for example) and inclusive of the work of some of today's best contemporary Christian artists (Amy Grant, Carolyn Arends, Steven Curtis Chapman, Jars of Clay, Rebecca St. James), the music of our band is one of the most exciting and substantive gifts that SUNDAY NIGHT has to offer.

Of course, in order to create quality music, the band requires a technical team. These are the people who oversee and manage the sound and lighting at SUNDAY NIGHT. In the course of nearly four years, we have assembled a team of "techies" who are as devoted as they are talented. Each week, they spend long hours preparing our sanctuary for the service and making sure that the band sounds as good as it can sound. SUNDAY NIGHT would not happen without their hard work.

Nonnegotiable Number 9: Grounded in the Discipline of Prayer

Nonnegotiable Number 10: Heartfelt Christian Commitment from All Worship Participants and Planners

Little needs to be said about the centrality of prayer and Christian commitment in the development of any new worship service. Quite simply, prayer and commitment are the foundation on which all worship is built. I am reminded of that truth every single week when our SUNDAY NIGHT worship team gathers for "prayer huddle" immediately prior to the service. There is always a profound sense of Presence in those huddles, a sense of Presence that keeps us humble, attentive, and focused upon our task. And behind that moment there is a blanket of prayer and committed action all week leading up to SUNDAY NIGHT.

Nonnegotiable Number 11: Thematic Foundation for Every Worship Service

Thematic development, I believe, is critically important to the success of any contemporary worship service. Ours is an image-oriented, theme-responsive, postmodern culture, filled with people who crave the existential idea—the lived-out, relationally embodied theme of every book they read, every movie they watch, every meeting they attend. There is a widespread cultural hunger for what Lewis H. Lapham describes as "the best that can be said in small space on short notice."[13]

I have learned that seekers approach a worship service with a craving for religious experience related to a need for a theme. Each one of our contemporary services, therefore, revolves around a thematic focus. The following are some of our SUNDAY NIGHT themes during the last year:

"What Does It Mean to Be Christian?" (seven-part Lenten series)

"CHOOSING WISELY: Things to Remember in the Search for a Spouse" (three parts)

"Living an Abundant Life" (four parts)

"Listening for a Whispering God in a Shouting World" (two parts)

"The Holiness of the Single Life"

"SACRED INTIMACY: Sexual Ethics from a Biblical Perspective"

"What Difference Does Prayer Make?"
"Why Bother Being Part of a Church?"
"The God Who Chose Infancy Over Infantry" (Christmas)
"What Is the Holy Spirit, Anyway?" (Pentecost)
"Making Time for Holy Encounters" (Transfiguration Sunday)
"The King and I" (Christ the King Sunday)
"Why Does God Seem to Be Hidden?"
"Dear God, My Family Is Falling Apart. Can You Please Help?"
"How Do I Move on from This Broken Relationship?"
(three parts)
"Honoring Our Marital Promises" (four parts)
"Approaching the Manger Rightly" (four-part Advent series)
"The Cost of Discipleship"
"The Divine Exclamation Point" (Easter)

I plan these themes six months at a time. I then pass them on to our music and drama teams, thereby ensuring that, in each worship service, the preaching, music, and drama will be grounded in the same theme. I have found that such thematic development brings about a powerful sense of cohesion and consistency in the context of SUNDAY NIGHT.

Something must be right about these nonnegotiables. The average attendance at SUNDAY NIGHT is approximately 350 people and the service is not yet four years old. Its impact on Christ Church (and this preacher) has been profound. Each SUNDAY NIGHT is an adventure in hospitality. Each SUNDAY NIGHT is an opportunity for Christ Church to open its heart and its doors to a group of seekers who are desperate for the salvation that only Christ can provide.

Conclusion: "More Like a Movie Theater Than a Museum"

I conclude by articulating a question that has often come my way: Can seeker-sensitive worship coexist with more traditional forms of worship? The answer, I believe, is a qualified "YES!" I am part of a church whose senior pastor has given SUNDAY NIGHT his highest affirmation and support; whose organist and music director see the SUNDAY NIGHT Band not as competition, but as an important component of the church's overall music ministry; whose staff and congregation look upon SUNDAY NIGHT not as an intrusion on the established order, but as a great place to bring their unchurched friends. In short, I am part of a progressive congregation eager to create cutting-edge worship that resonates with praise and Truth in the advent of a new millennium.

When I ponder the number of genuine seekers I meet in the context of my ministry, it becomes clear to me that the question of whether or not seeker-sensitive worship can coexist with traditional worship is moot. The real question is, Can we afford *not* to offer both traditional and contemporary worship opportunities in growing intergenerational, culturally responsive, multiple congregations?

A divorced man sought me out following a recent SUNDAY NIGHT service. He had an expression of sadness on his face that could not help revealing his temperament. "You know," he said, "after my divorce, I didn't feel comfortable attending my church anymore because my ex-wife was still there. And so I started searching around. I came to SUNDAY NIGHT for the first time about a month ago and I've been here ever since."

"I'm glad," I responded. "But tell me, what is it about this service that you find particularly meaningful?"

"It's a number of things," he answered. "But maybe most of all, this church feels more like a movie theater than a museum. And I'm at a place in life where 'movie theater church' makes a whole lot more sense. It's more relevant and relational. It's more real."

If the church of Jesus Christ wants to be at its most articulate in the proclamation of the gospel, then it must resist the temptation to become a museum of saints in a movie

140

theater culture. John Wesley was prophetic enough in his cultural discernment to recognize the need for worship that moved beyond the walls of Anglican architecture. My earnest prayer is that the contemporary church will become just as bold in its vision, and just as visionary in its worship, as the early Methodist enthusiasts.

CHAPTER SIX

Circuit Riding in the Twenty-First Century

Robert Duncan Jr.

If the technology that fueled the Protestant Reformation was the printing press, and the product was "The Book," the technology that is fueling the Postmodern Reformation is the microprocessor, and the product is "The Net."
— *Leonard Sweet* [1]

We are in the middle of a new Reformation, the social and religious transformation from a modern to a postmodern global culture. The innovative use of the book in the Protestant Reformation is being replayed in innovative uses of new electronic publishing sources. The instant availability of information around the globe is a new reality. The potential for spreading the gospel to mass audiences has never been greater. We have an opportunity to redeem the technology of the culture and use it for ministry in the electronification of the church. For Wesleyans, electronic circuit riding in the twenty-first century is a new form of evangelism and mission.

How Did We Get Here?

First came the Classical or Agrarian Age. The contents of the gospel were entrusted to the hands of scribes who codified the oral traditions by which families passed the faith from one generation to the next. New understanding was limited to specific geographic areas, and new thought traveled slowly. People often lived and died without leaving their village or province. Their worldview was provential. They relied on others to maintain the faith.

Then came the Modern Age, a time of reason and enlightenment. This transition brought with it the Protestant Reformation. Science produced technological progress and the church found the power of the printed word. The world and the church changed forever. Steady progress in transportation and communication led to colonization and conversion in remote areas of our planet. We moved toward becoming a global village, but information remained a print-based medium, with television ministry occasionally reaching the masses.

A Postmodern Reformation is now underway! The rapid change we are facing is the completion of the Information Age. Electronic technology is building on the use of the transistor and computer chip to create a worldwide network of complex computers. As we face the reality of the Postmodern Reformation, the gospel will need to be presented in powerful new ways. The possibility for interactive, two-way communication and information already exists. Through videoconferencing software, for example, we can move back to a one-on-one sharing of the gospel without the limitations of time or distance.

Churches that embrace the technology of the Information Age will be transformed and experience unlimited possibilities in their ministry. This does not mean that all of our pastors need to be technopreachers or cyberevangelists. The reality of this reformation is that the skills of the Information

Age are already present in each congregation through mobilizing laity. By recognizing these skills as new "spiritual gifts and graces" pastors can grant permission to their members to bring their secular skills into the ministry of the electronic church. This will broaden our understanding of how we use our gifts in service to God.

The electronification of the church is not a new phenomenon; it started when the first electric lightbulb was brought inside the church. It has continued with the evolution of electronics as a global industry, and has made quantum leaps with each new technological breakthrough. What is new is the speed in which technology is being advanced, the drop in price for new technology, and the ability of this new technology to improve communication and interactivity.

Over the centuries, the church has made use of all sorts of technology, including electric lights, electric organs, slide projectors, overhead transparencies, television and radio, filmstrips and movies, printing presses, mimeograph machines, photocopiers, typewriters, and computers and printers. Oftentimes the church has lagged behind the technology of the day. We have resisted technology, condemned technology, and feared technology.

Today we are faced with the wonderful opportunity of using technology to reformat our timeless message. Polished presentations were once almost exclusively the domain of big business or government. The cost of fancy production left the church out in the dark. This is not true anymore. The advances of new information technology have made the New Reformation possible. We can now present the gospel in new ways and accomplish ministry through new forms of media.

Much of the technology can be used in the areas of education and worship. The new interactivity of Information Age-technology brings the possibility of new applications in visitation and communication ministries. For example, professionals may be able to join together online during the day for a cyber discussion or a Bible study. This same technology can also be applied to youth, college, young adults, parents, and homebound parishioners for *"high-tech, high-touch"* ministry.

Technology can also be used to reach unchurched people where they are in a technoculture. Once we have engaged persons of this culture they expect "their" culture to be present in "our" church. If it is absent, we will not be embraced and we will have missed an important part of what it means to be the church in our age.

The point is that we can reach more people with more spiritual content than ever before in ways that make the message come alive for them. We can also use technology to free up *administrative time* for *ministry time.*

Where Do We Find This New Technology?

Shifts in Communication

Oral→→→Visual→→→Written→→→Printed→→→Electronic

This new technology was not developed specifically for the church's ministry. It was developed for other aspects of our society and culture; namely, military, education, business, and (yes) the sex industry. However, the development of new technology and its application is not limited to secular use.

In order to embrace this technology, the church will have to interpret its value and provide a context for how it can be used in the work of the ministry. A new contextual understanding of ministry can then serve as a filter to help identify what technology can be integrated into the ministry of the church.

Technology should not be used just because it is available, nor should it be avoided because it has been developed by the secular world. The potential for ministry is not found in the technology per se; rather, the potential is found in the application and integration of technology in ministry. The argument here is based on prioritizing what ministry the church is engaged in and then looking for the best available technology to accomplish or implement that ministry.

For example, we can look to business applications to improve the way the church operates administratively. This includes word processing, accounting, database management, scheduling, personal information managers, and contact management software.

Likewise, for communications we can look to graphics software, desktop publishing software and equipment, e-mail programs, phone trees, voice mail, fax, print, and audio and video technologies.

Administration and communications are common examples of how the types of technologies that have been created  for the secular society can be claimed for the ministry of the church. We are faced with the opportunity and challenge to look at our core ministry areas such as pastoral care, preaching, worship, and then adapt available technologies for ministry.

The World Wide Web

Ian Morrison reported in his book, *The Second Curve,* that at least "40 percent of all American households have a computer, and some 40 percent of those are connected by modem to the outside world. An estimated 50 percent of U.S. workers now routinely use a computing device at their jobs."[2] Households with school-age children and households with retirees comprise the two most important markets for the computer industry.

146

The Internet and World Wide Web have gone through enormous change since their early beginnings in the 1960s. Web pages now are available to everyone and every organization. The American Bible Society has launched a multimillion dollar program to give every church the opportunity to have its own website. Many denominations already have similar programs in place. New programs make preparing web pages as easy as using your word processing program. In fact, some word processing programs now include web publishing as a printing option.

The Web has gone from a billboard-oriented medium that allowed businesses and individuals to announce: "We are here!" to a dynamic medium that provides limited interactive information on demand. IBM launched an ad campaign celebrating work done on the Web. You can now balance your checkbook, order books, or buy cars, computers, airline tickets, and flowers right from your keyboard.

And it isn't stopping there! The Web is rapidly evolving toward more interactivity and multilayered, multidimensional, and multilinked sharing of information. First there was e-mail, then list servers, then bulletin boards, then chat rooms, and now video conferencing live on the Web. The circuit rider of eighteenth-century American Methodism has become the cybersurfer of the twenty-first-century electronic frontier.

Transitions

horseback $\rightarrow \rightarrow \rightarrow \rightarrow \rightarrow \rightarrow \rightarrow \rightarrow \rightarrow \rightarrow$ internet
saddlebag $\rightarrow \rightarrow \rightarrow \rightarrow \rightarrow \rightarrow \rightarrow \rightarrow \rightarrow \rightarrow$ laptop computer
itinerancy $\rightarrow \rightarrow \rightarrow \rightarrow \rightarrow \rightarrow \rightarrow \rightarrow \rightarrow \rightarrow$ online access
circuit riding $\rightarrow \rightarrow \rightarrow \rightarrow \rightarrow \rightarrow \rightarrow \rightarrow \rightarrow$ fiberoptics
rider $\rightarrow \rightarrow \rightarrow \rightarrow \rightarrow \rightarrow \rightarrow \rightarrow \rightarrow \rightarrow \rightarrow$ surfer

For these gifts to take root we need to become change leaders for a changing church, speed up our planning processes, think in new ways, build upon our knowledge base, and transform our ministry for the twenty-first century.

Because of this new interactivity, the church of the New Reformation has at least four new gifts for ministry:

- better tools
- more knowledge
- more choices
- greater power

We now have the opportunity to reenvision ministry by rethinking our roles in the work and ministry of the church. This will effect:

- worship
- Christian education
- administration
- missions
- congregational care

Worship

Since we now have a framework for understanding the potential for circuit riding in the twenty-first century, let's consider what new form ministry will take. And why not consider mobilizing a techno-gifted lay minister to implement some of the following enhancements to Sunday worship?

Gathering

Announcements in Narthex on TV Consider using the technology that is so popular in hotel and convention centers to announce events and meeting-room assignments. Attach a scan converter to the office computer and run CATV cable to a TV located in the narthex. Presentation software (like Powerpoint) will allow you to creatively replace bulletin boards. A flatbed scanner or digital camera will even allow you to add photos to the presentation. Attach a WAV file to the presentation to add the sounds of ministry: the choir or church school program.

Local Browsers for Ministry Information Use a web page design program to develop specific web pages for your church ministries. Put these pages on your church server and allow local access using your browser. This works like the Internet without the issues surrounding logging on to an Internet Service Provider.

Visitor Kiosk with Local Browser and Video Dedicate a computer and install it in a kiosk that allows for screen and mouse access only. Put your church web pages containing general information on the computer hard drive. This visitor kiosk can then be used to surf (using local browser technology) for ministry information and events that are planned or that have taken place. A fun alternative is to design a kids' kiosk to "teach" about faith during fellowship hour!

Bulletin

The printed bulletin serves to provide a structure for the congregation to worship together. Computer-generated video projected onto screens or monitors as the service unfolds meets this same purpose in worship. It also allows the members of the congregation to be more aware of their surroundings and more in touch with one another as they get away from the insulation of individual bulletins.

Contemporary Worship

Many churches would like to add a contemporary service but do not believe that they have the ability to support the music needed for such a service. There are a number of technological advances that make this dream a possibility for every local church. A few examples are:

Solo Music Using a Soundtrack Christian bookstores now stock CDs and cassette tapes that are mastered with only the soundtrack. The live soloist then sings to the music, much in the same way that music is now recorded on multiple sound tracks.

"Live Music" It is also possible for a single musician to add a rich sound to worship using a single MIDI keyboard. The MIDI can be programmed to provide for the sound of an entire band. When tied to a computer it can also "play back" the music that is most frequently used in worship (a great substitute organist).

New Sound Systems The right sound equipment is a prerequisite to implementing the above examples and many more new worship options. Wireless mics, sub-bass woofers, surround sound, mixing decks, and proper speakers will make or break this effort. Resist at all costs the use of portable CD or tape players to support soloists or choirs.

Set the Stage The extensive use of drama in contemporary worship is also enhanced by the use of sound and lighting systems that have been transformed by technological advances. It is possible to control lighting and sound by computer and integrate a wide variety of audio and video applications. This allows contemporary worship to have a very finished and professional quality in its drama presentations.

Preaching

> *"The Computer Screen is the stained glass window of our time."*
>
> —*Leonard I. Sweet* [3]

Professors of homiletics have told aspiring preachers to tell the story and provide "visual" images to allow the sermon to come to life. These "visual" images have been limited to verbal descriptions and an occasional "show-and-tell" prop. We now have the capacity to project an image of the painting, the quote from the book, the clip from the movie, the pictures from the mission trip, the images of the Holy Land, key sermon points in bullet format (new meaning to the three-point sermon) or the biblical map that brings the sermon to life.

Christian Education

Another area of the church's ministry that is easily adapted to electronification is Christian education—the teaching ministries of the church. One of the greatest potentials for this application is generating congregation-specific materials rather than using generic materials.

Congregation Specific Curriculum

Teaching about the life, history, beliefs, and practices of a local congregation is becoming more critical as we recognize the mobility of the membership in our congregations. Not only do we have a lack of historical continuity, we also have a blending of denominational values and the understanding of fundamental beliefs. One way to enhance teaching is to convert presentation graphics using a scan converter and interlace them with video for use in VHS format. This can be used in classes, visits, or self-paced education in settings like:

- new-member class
- confirmation class
- baptism counseling
- wedding counseling
- funeral counseling

Computer Assisted Learning

One of the best ways to teach is to use a format that is recognized and accepted by the student population. Our children are products of the Information Age and they expect to learn using technology as an integral part of the process. Her are three examples of how to use "their" technology in Christian education:

1. Give the members of your church school or confirmation class a Bible: a PC Bible Atlas or a PC Bible instead of a printed Bible. Likewise, consider placing a PC

151

equipped with a suite of Bible, Hebrew, or Greek translations, multimedia Bible stories, CD music, and mapping programs in every classroom.

2. Take field trips without even leaving the classroom. Many web sites now have live video feeds for visitors to use while exploring their site.

3. Instead of doing a pen pal project with a missionary, try e-mail, video mail, or video conferencing by means of the Internet.

Chat Rooms for Adult Learning

Commuting and changing work patterns create serious challenges to the church offering Christian education to its members. Chat rooms are an option to overcoming distance and daily schedules. These allow church members to join together for "online" discussions when they cannot physically be together. Applications include:

- noon Bible study
- parenting classes
- support groups
- youth ministry
- young-adult ministry

Web-Based Resources for Ministry Teams

How can we provide training and teaching resources for our Christian education team? The old model brought them together at the church for a Saturday morning meeting where we distributed teacher packets of Sunday school materials.

A new electronic possibility would be to place materials on the Web for our teaching team to access. We could also provide access to other churches and share information with them. This material might include articles on teaching styles, activities for class, or customized curriculum. Everything would be available for easy access regardless of time or distance.

By the same token, training materials and resources offered to fellowship groups in the church, including devotional guides, denominational materials, leadership manuals, or group activities could be made available as well for:

- women's groups
- men's groups
- youth groups
- singles ministries
- single parents

Church Management in the Technological Age

Church administration is one of the areas where the adaptation of business technologies can be most easily accomplished, especially in the areas of communications and printed materials. Here are a few ideas:

Bulletins

It is now possible to produce high-quality, computer-generated bulletins in almost every church. With new software, printers, copiers, and electronically connected commercial printing services, any church can now produce the same quality bulletin that was once reserved for large churches.

You can now add color and quality graphics at minimal cost. The proper use of these two ingredients can make your print materials come alive. They can also support and add to the worship experience.

One unique possibility for "bridging" our print and Web materials is to cross-reference them. For example, you could list your Web page address, provide a link to the sermon that has been "Net published," or a link to the choir's anthem that has been "Net published" and is available for purchase on the Internet. Now your worship elements are available worldwide, not only for people to read about, but to experience directly from their screen and integrated CD stereo system. Your Web ministry then makes the transition from billboard to interactive options.

Newsletters

The same publishing technology available for bulletins can also be used to produce professional quality newsletters. The expense for this technology is now so affordable that nearly any size church can produce eye-catching newsletters.

What are the implications? You can transform your newsletter with electronic graphics, utilize digital photography, accept articles via e-mail, "Net publish" the monthly newsletter on your Web page, and distribute the newsletter via an e-mail list server, or offer it as a download option from your website.

Calendars

In the modern period the church relied on preprinted or formatted calendar blanks to print its monthly or weekly calendar. A major drawback was the rigid format that did not allow adequate space for Sunday programming. A second drawback was the time lead needed for the calendar production. With the electronification of the church we can overcome these drawbacks and others like them. We now can produce custom formats for the church calendar. Make it a point to use the best software and printer available to you and be sure to include graphics, color, and photos. Post it on your web page and include hyper links to more information about each of the activities and the groups sponsoring them. Provide e-mail links to request information or make reservations. Send copies and notices to focus groups via e-mail. Consider sending copies with press releases by fax and e-mail.

How to Work Smarter, Not Harder, in Church Administration

A major goal of technological church management is to reduce the time we spend in administrative details. An increase in administrative efficiency and effectiveness provides more time for hands-on ministry. The modern reality was informed by process meetings and strategic planning. The postmodern potential is realized by fewer meetings and chordic preparedness.

Meeting Ideas

Technology in the church should be able to support whatever aspect of ministry in which we are currently engaged. Here are four examples of how we can use technology to increase administrative efficiency and effectiveness:

- use e-mail to send meeting reminders and include an agenda
- use presentation graphics for reports
- build a meeting notebook for all participants
- consider online meetings that allow for multiple tasks

Registration Pads

To encourage the integration of technology and ministry, all aspects of church life must be addressed. Some churches seek to improve communications by using e-mail whenever possible, and therefore include space for an e-mail address in their registration pads placed in the pew.

Print Ads

Include your Web and e-mail addresses in all church advertising and promotion. This informs readers about how to get more information and tells them about your interest in using postmodern technologies in your ministry.

Staff Projects

The postmodern reality is directed by team collaboration. This structure does not require face-to-face contact on a daily basis or the entire *team* working together on all projects at all times. Individual efforts and proceedings in a coordinated team process can accomplish much more than the group working together in unison. To help keep the *team* coordinated, there are a number of technological possibilities including the use of a local area network, e-mail, or whiteboard software to reduce or eliminate unnecessary meetings.

Ministry Involvement and Integration

How well do you share what is happening at your church? Consider using e-mail and community bulletin boards to share what is happening at your church and include other information in your calendar, newsletter, or web site.

Congregational Care Ideas

Directories

- Publish the church directory on the Web and include e-mail.
- Use a password for the privacy of your membership.
- Include membership photos of church families.

Internet Visitation

- Use the Internet to visit members who you cannot visit in person.
- Link to military personnel and college students from the church wherever they are by means of video chat.
- Encourage the youth group to form a young adult cyber club to stay in touch while they are at school.
- Bring homebound members together for fellowship opportunities online.

- Visit business travelers through e-mail while they are on the road.

E-Mail Interaction

- Make it easier for church members to ask faith-based questions by encouraging e-mail communication.

List Servers

- Have each ministry area develop a list of interested persons and include their e-mail addresses or fax numbers for regular distribution of information.
- Send messages to the participants in your Christian education program or small-group ministry.

Mission

Ministry Concerns

When I present to pastors the need to pursue an "electronification" of the church, I almost always hear three questions:

1. Are new skills required?
2. Is interpersonal contact different?
3. Is this appropriate for smaller congregations?

Here's how I respond:

New Skills. Yes, we need to be "retooled" as change leaders for a changing church. However, there are adequate numbers of lay leaders with the technical skills required for the church's mission in this new reformation. We may have to look to nontraditional places to find these gifted persons. Further, once we have found them they may need help envisioning the call God has placed on their lives and them-

157

selves in ministry. Having established that connection, they will, on their own, want to share this new information. Then, we need only to give them permission and freedom to spread the gospel in new ways.

Interpersonal Contact The goal of using electronics in ministry is to be on the front lines of ministry. Technology is not a substitute for ministry as we know it. Rather, it is just another tool to reach persons who would not otherwise be reached, enabling ministry in a new context.

Congregational Size The need to use electronics in ministry is greatest in large and small congregations. In large congregations, it makes keeping in contact with all members possible. In small congregations it multiplies the efforts of the few to reach out to the many. The electronification of the church is only one way the church can live out its ministry. We need to use all the tools available to proclaim the gospel to a needy and hungry world.[4]

Economic Concerns

I often hear the objection that the technology needed for the electronification of the church is unaffordable. I counter by saying we cannot afford *not* to implement new technologies into our ministries. I can also make a case for the ability to implement cutting-edge technology without breaking the bank. Drew Theological School's **Logon@Drew** website is an illustration of this principle.[5]

At Drew, in less than a month we were able to design and post an interactive education web site. We did this on a virtual server using an "off campus" hosting service. We did this to illustrate the process for a local church to implement a Web-based ministry. For less than $600 we were able to present a wide variety of offerings on the web. All of our offerings included *interactive* components, including auto respond e-mail, online registration, downloadable lectures, threaded discussions, chat rooms and *CU-SeeMe*© video conferencing. With the exception of the *CU-SeeMe*© technology, all of this was available as freeware or shareware on the Web. We designed and posted the pages using *Adobe PageMill*. In preparation for United Methodist annual conferences, we produced a new video for use at lunches and display tables. We made a Corel presentation and converted it to videotape using a scan converter. For presentation graphics in worship, try converting presentation graphics to 35 mm slides. Every church can come up with an old projector!

This chapter has addressed the reality and possibilities for ministry in the Postmodern Reformation. The new reality facing the church is one of enhanced communication tools and expectations for good communication. This is a time when we can reach more people and share the gospel in more compelling ways than ever before. The guiding principle is that the postmodern world is one that offers both/and not either/or options.

I invite you to *live* what we have been recommending in this chapter: Get interactive! Join us online and post your responses to this chapter by sending an e-mail to RDuncan@drew.edu. Together we can ride the circuit in the twenty-first century . . . online.

CHAPTER SEVEN

Three Streams, One River

Michael J. Christensen

There is a river whose streams make glad the city of God.

(Psalm 46:4)

Toward a New Ordering of the Ministry of the Baptized

How can ministerial leadership (clergy) move the people of God (laity) from the baptismal font into the full flow of ministry[1] in the church and mission[2] in the world? The "river vision" in Psalm 46 offers a biblical image of happy, healing waters that make glad the city.[3] A spiritual interpretation of the river vision provides a metaphorical basis for the ministry of the baptized, ordered not around traditional roles and distinctions between clergy and laity, but rather around spiritual gifts, graces, passions, callings and streams of ministry.

The New Testament church was largely built on the charismatic leadership of the apostles and their successors. This ancient order gradually gave rise to clericalism and institutionalized ministry. The modern church, after a brief revival and affirmation of the priesthood of all believers in the Protestant Reformation, preserved the classical distinction between clergy and laity. This "two stream" model of church may now be abandoned in favor of a new model: A "three streams, one river" church in which the people of God claim their priesthood, find their passion for ministry, and flow within the stream of their gifts and calling in the New Reformation of the Laity.

What I envision for *TheNextChurch* is one order of Christians with a threefold ministry of the baptized. The three major streams of ministry in the one river of God, I believe, are *community, worship,* and *mission. Laos,* the people of God, are called to swim in the river and express themselves primarily in one particular stream of ministry, while participating in all three. No longer must we continue to call people in the worship stream "clergy" and those in the mission stream "laity." Rather, all the baptized in Christ may be ordained as ministers, called and equipped to swim in a particular tributary in the one river of God. It is an ancient, biblical vision, yet one that requires a revival of emphasis from time to time. The dawn of the third millennium of Christendom is a time that is ripe for the river vision.

The River Vision

Rivers in many religions, historically and theologically, are seen as sacred sites and places of pilgrimage. During my first pilgrimage to India in 1984, while in search of the source of the Ganges River, I found myself alone at dusk in Varanasi, on the banks of the river. I was meditating on the sacred qualities of the great *Ganga* (Ganges), which the Hindus personify as a god. The river begins, I was told, high in the Himalayas at a glacier point known as Hardwar, where gods and gurus are thought to dwell. There the water is cold and fresh and clear as crystal. But as the head waters flow down the mountains, they are joined by tributaries that eventually form the one great river *Ganga*. As the river flows through crowded cities, like Varanasi, it becomes polluted and finally empties out into the sea. People still drink the water as it flows past them, hoping to be blessed or healed of their diseases. When the devoted in India die, they want their ashes to be scattered on the waters of the Ganges in the hope of immortality. What I witnessed in Varanasi were thousands of pilgrims as they arrived before dawn to bathe in the sacred waters, their faces to the east. I watched them dip three times as they said their prayers, cup their hands, and drink.

For hours I watched, pondering to myself: How can people bathe in such pollution? The muddy waters of the Ganges cannot possibly bring life and wholeness. People dip but are they healed? They drink but are they satisfied? They make pilgrimage but do they find God at its source? They die and their ashes are scattered on the river, but do they find eternal life? Yet "there is a river whose streams make glad the city of God" (Psalm 46:4)! Its clear crystal streams are meant to bring healing and hope, gladness and joy, to those who dip and drink its waters. How to channel this river of God to the suffering city of humanity? How to restore the life-giving flow from the holy mountain? How to revive the river whose streams are meant to refresh and fulfill God's people?

My reflection on the Ganges carried me to Ezekiel's prophecy of a river that has its source on Mount Zion, at the throne of the Temple of God (Ezekiel 47). There its waters are pure as crystal, intended to heal the people who drink from its streams. The sacred river flows down the mountain past the city and toward the Dead Sea. When it enters the sea of stagnant waters, the water will become fresh. "Swarms of living creatures will live *wherever the river flows*" (Ezekiel 47:9 NIV; emphasis mine).

> Fruit trees of all kinds will grow on both banks of the river. Their leaves will not wither, nor will their fruit fail. Every

month they will bear, because the water from the sanctuary flows to them. Their fruit will serve for food and their leaves for healing. (Ezekiel 47:12 NIV)

There is a river whose streams refresh the people of God. Those who bathe in this river, drink from the streams, eat of the fruit, and use the leaves from the trees, shall be healed. What a vision! What does it mean?

Richard Foster has helped me appreciate the mystical depths of Ezekiel's vision of the river of God and its relevance to contemporary spirituality and compassionate ministry. In a 1998 pastoral letter, he writes:

> Everything surrounding this vision is about walls and stones, bricks and mortar. Then, suddenly, right in the midst of these static images, Ezekiel sees water pouring out from under the altar; the River of God flowing with life and power. It is a vision which looks both backward and forward: backward to the river flowing from the garden of Eden; forward to "the river of the water of life" which is flowing eternally through the middle of the New Jerusalem. (Genesis 2:10; Revelation 22:1)[4]

The angel in Ezekiel's vision escorts the prophet outside the temple and shows him how the river of God flows out beyond the altar (where only priests were allowed) and even beyond the perimeter of the courts of the temple (where the Gentiles lurked). Not only does the river overflow the Jew and Gentile boundaries, but clergy and lay distinctions. "This, you see," writes Foster, "is a River of life that simply cannot be confined to any religious system, no matter how worthy."[5]

The River of God is flowing today, Foster proclaims in *Streams of Living Water.* No one can stop it, and no one can contain it. "It is a deep river of divine intimacy, a powerful river of holy living, a dancing river of jubilation in the Spirit, and a broad river of unconditional love for all peoples."[6]

The historical background of Ezekiel 47 is the exile of Israel to Babylon. In 586 B.C.E. the Babylonians destroyed the city of Jerusalem and burned the Temple to the ground. The reference to the source of the river at the temple throne is poetic metaphor, derived no doubt from the ritual pouring of water by priests at the Temple, for no literal springs flow from the altar. The river image represents the tranquility and blessing the city of Jerusalem once enjoyed under God's protection, and which one day will be restored (cf. other river images in Scripture, including: Genesis 2:10; Psalm 46:4, Isaiah 66:12; Ezekiel 47; Amos 5:24; Zechariah 14:8; and Revelation 22:1).

Israel was captive in Babylon, her Temple destroyed; but in the midst of exile and national despair God gave Ezekiel a series of millennial visions of the resurrection, restoration, and renewal of the city of God. These visions are preserved in twelve chapters (Ezekiel 37–48) and also apply to the church of Jesus Christ in postmodern captivity. In the existential valley of dry bones, hope for renewal can be raised from the ashes of despair. There is a river whose streams empower the *laos* of God. And the promise is that *wherever the river flows,* new life will come!

Jesus announced the New Age of the Spirit on the last day of the Feast of Tabernacles when he declared to the woman at Jacob's well: "Let anyone who is thirsty come to me, and let the one who believes in me drink. As the scripture has said, 'Out of the believer's heart shall flow rivers of living water" (John 7:37-38). When the Day of Pentecost had come, the gifts and manifestations of the Spirit were given to the followers of Jesus, first to the Jewish but also to the Gentile believers (Acts 2). In trying to explain the phenomenon of the Spirit being poured out on all the believers that day, regardless of race, gender, or nationality, Peter quoted from the prophet Joel:

> Even on my servants, both men and women, I will pour out my Spirit in those days, and they will prophesy. (Acts 2:18 NIV)

The Protestant doctrine of the priesthood of believers and equality of roles in the Body of Christ is based on this initial outpouring of the Spirit—this new temple and river of life— at Pentecost. There remains a river of the Spirit whose ever flowing streams refresh the people of God. John of Patmos, a disciple of Jesus and partaker of the Spirit of Pentecost, shares Ezekiel's vision of the mighty river. As he describes it in Revelation, the waters of the river of God are "clear as crystal, flowing from the throne of God and of the Lamb down the middle of the great street of the city." On the side of the river is the tree of life bearing twelve crops of fruit. "And the leaves of the tree are for the healing of the nations" (Revelation 22:1, 2).

The river, then, is an eschatological vision of the heart of God and fruit of ministry when all of the world shall feast. The river of God is meant to flow to and through believers and bring healing and wholeness to broken lives in the city of need. God's intention is for *all* to share in *shalom*—the peace, joy, justice, healing, and wholeness that comes from freely drinking the water of life. But the river has become dammed up, obstructed by sin and injustice, and polluted by exclusivity and privilege. Who will purify the polluted streams and restore the life-giving flow? The church of Jesus Christ, the *laos* of God, the priesthood of believers are God's chosen means of purification, restoration, and spiritual access. "We are therefore Christ's ambassadors, as though God were making his appeal through us" (2 Corinthians 5:20 NIV). Our mission on earth is to find out and cooperate with what God is doing in the world, until God's kingdom has fully come. The future reality to which the river points is a present vocation for the church in its prophetic ministry of justice, redemption, and reconciliation.

For this purpose we have been called, gifted, equipped, and empowered. While some are called to preach and teach, others are called to point and prophesy. With many tongues, all are called to stir up the stale waters of the church and society where a reservoir of life-giving water has been collected and prevented from flowing to places of need. In the New Reformation of the Laity, the people of God are rising up in opposition to clerical privilege, episcopal power, and ecclesial exclusivity in ministry. They are upsetting the status quo, challenging authority, opposing the principalities, and demanding an end to the damming and polluting of the river of God meant to make glad the city. Priest and prophet, laity and clergy, active and contemplative, together we work and pray: "Thy kingdom come, thy will be done." And we will not rest until that day when the ancient vision has been fulfilled, and the streams of living water once again flow from God's inclusive heart to every human heart in need. That's my understanding of the vision!

Three Streams, One River

The river vision is fed by three healing streams, each of which has its function and contribution to the saving work of God. Just as the Ganges River of India begins at a sacred mountain spring, incorporates tributaries, and becomes one river, so the river of life in Scripture has its source at God's holy mountain throne, incorporates tributaries, and becomes one river. This *"three streams, one river"* philosophy of ministry that has undergirded my theology of lay ministry for over two decades. It has informed my priorities, programs, and structures in my urban and international ministries. It has kept me biblically balanced, spiritually focused, and less likely to burn out when the waters are troubled. It has allowed me the freedom to trust the priesthood of believers as God's chosen provision to fulfill the mission, and to let go of the illusion that I, as clergy, must do all the work myself.

I first encountered a *"three streams, one river"* approach to ministry at the Church of the Apostles (Episcopal) in Charleston, Virginia, in the early 1980s. The rector, Fr. Renny Scott, was active in the charismatic renewal movement of the 1970s and 1980s, and sought to affirm and integrate the divergent streams of ecclesial tradition in his large and growing parish. Renny taught that the river vision of Ezekiel and John represents three great streams of divine revelation that can be applied to traditional distinctions: in the *Godhead* (Father, Son, and Holy Spirit), in *church history* (Catholic, Protestant, and charismatic), in *church structure* (celebration, congregational life, and cell groups), in worship styles (liturgical, formal, and free form), and in *standards of orthodoxy*. He supported this teaching with a verse from 1 John 5:8—"And there are three that bear witness in earth, the Spirit, and the water, and the blood: and these three agree in one" (KJV). When all three witnesses or streams flow as one river, they "make glad the city."

Godhead: The three streams of the same river can be associated with three primal images (wind, water, blood) representing the Holy Trinity flowing out to bring wholeness to humanity. Each person of the Triune God fulfills a distinctive role in the salvation of the body, soul, and spirit. The Father is the one who "gives all [persons] life and breath and everthing else. . . . For in him we live and move and have our being" (Acts 17:25, 28 NIV). The Son is the one who "was pierced for our transgressions . . . crushed for our iniquities . . . and by his wounds we are healed" (Isaiah 53:5 NIV). The Spirit is the counselor, comforter, intercessor, and sustainer in life and ministry. "For God did not give us a spirit of timidity, but a spirit of power, of love and self-discipline" (2 Timothy 1:7 NIV).

Church History: Though the river of God is one, three streams flow out of the Trinity, each a guardian tradition in church history. The stream of the Father Almighty, maker of heaven and earth, finds its expression in church history as Roman Catholicism with its emphasis on divine mystery, blood sacrifice, sacramentalism, and liturgical worship. Protestants, on the other hand, tend to swim in the stream of the *Word*—the Lord Jesus Christ, Son of the Living God. They emphasize the humanity of Christ over divine mystery, water baptism over blood sacrifice, Word over sacrament,

167

and faith in Jesus over works that glorify the Father. Charismatics, it would follow, sail in the stream called the Spirit, embracing community life, personal experience, and spontaneous worship and celebration.

Church Structure: The basic structure of the Catholic stream is the neighborhood parish. Each local church, connected to a hierarchical tradition, takes responsibility for all the Catholic families in a particular neighborhood. Protestant structure is more regional, egalitarian, and centered around the preached word. The parish is defined less geographically and more by whosoever finds their way to the church, the table, or to the ministry center. Preaching points, known as churches, may or may not be community based, but reach out widely in proclamation and mission. Charismatic structure, on the other hand, is relatively loose. Lots of small groups and large celebrations cluster around a charismatic leader or dynamic movement. The primary unit is the cell group of spiritual accountability and fellowship in the Spirit.

Worship Styles: Each stream, it seems, has its own music and style of worship. Catholics like to chant the psalms while Protestants generally enjoy singing hymns. Charismatics, with outreached hands, tend to offer choruses of praise and thanksgiving. The apostle Paul recommends all three:

> Speak to one another with psalms, hymns and spiritual songs. Sing and make music in your heart to the Lord, always giving thanks to God the Father for everything, in the name of our Lord Jesus Christ. (Ephesians 5:19, 20 NIV)

Standards of Orthodoxy: The three steams also have three different standards of orthodoxy, all biblical, yet each often the cause of division in the Body of Christ. Catholics require *good works and character* as evidence of Christ's presence in a believer's life. "Thus, by their fruit you will recognize them" (Matthew 7:20 NIV). Protestants insist on *right belief* as the standard of orthodox faith. "That if you confess with your mouth, 'Jesus is Lord,' and believe in your heart that

God raised him from the dead, you will be saved" (Romans 10:9). For Protestants, especially evangelicals, it is not so much who you *are* and what you *do,* but what you *say* about Jesus that counts. For charismatics, the *gifts of the Spirit* are most important. "Now to each one the manifestation of the Spirit is given for the common good" (1 Corinthians 12 NIV). A person may do all the right things and say all the right words, but "test the spirits" to see whether that person has the Holy Spirit and thus belongs to God (1 John 4:1 NIV).

The chart below contrasts the three guardian traditions and the streams of emphases they tend to represent.

Three Streams, One River
Psalm 46:4

Father	Son	Holy Spirit
Blood	Water *(1 John 5:8)*	Spirit
Sacrifice	Cleansing	Renewal
Catholic/	Protestant/	Pentecostal/
Orthodox	Evangelical	Charismatic
Sacraments	Word	Experience
Psalms	Hymns	Spiritual Songs
Fruit/Works	Belief	Gifts
(Matthew 2:20)	*(Romans 10:9)*	*(1 Corinthians 12)*
Parish	Congregation	Cell
Worship	Community	Mission

From a two-stream church of clergy and laity to one order of Christians with the threefold ministry of the baptized.

Recognizing the guardian traditions of the three streams and the need for renewal through swimming cross-current.

Which stream is best: Catholic, Protestant, or charismatic? It all depends on where one begins. I learned to swim in the evangelical Protestant stream. I was "born again" at seven years of age, "sanctified" at fifteen, and was challenged to be a "witness for Christ" so that others would come to believe. During my high school and college years, I was attracted to the charismatic movement, which seemed to offer more power and spiritual vitality than I had in my own tradition. I discovered spiritual gifts, the power of prayer, and the joy of praise. During my seminary training, I studied with Fr. Henri Nouwen at Yale, and found myself attending daily Mass with the Catholics. I grew to love liturgy, reverence the Sacraments, and see the importance of good works and character. What brought these three streams together to form one river for me was the challenge of planting a new church in the city.

An exclusively evangelical Protestant stream proved to be too shallow. Protestantism, traditionally understood, tends to limit ministry to the proclamation of the Word, requiring only a confessional response from those who are attracted to the gift of preaching. Protestant worship is understood as attending church, singing preparatory hymns to a topical or expository sermon about how to live the Christian life, and responding personally with right belief. There is little sense of mystery, transcendence, or corporate participation in the glory of God.

The charismatic stream can be equally limiting in its emphasis on spiritual experiences, corporate praise rallies, and principles of personal piety and prosperity taught during worship times. The social mandate to feed the hungry, clothe the needy, and shelter the homeless is often missing. Missing too are the life-giving sacraments, apostolic tradition, and eucharistic worship.

Catholicism, though a more ancient, deeper, and satisfying stream, also has its shortcomings. Eastern Orthodoxy and Roman Catholicism, in my view, hold too tightly to church tradition for its own sake, accommodate too easily to the expectations of civil religion and politics, and trust too much in hierarchical judgments and papal authority. The ancient vision of transcendence is a treasure, but the attitude of triumphalism is a problem.

What finally came together for me was a threefold emphasis on ortho*doxy* (right worship), ortho*praxis* (right action), and ortho*cardia* (right heart). The church I planted sought to embody a *three-streams, one river* vision of Christianity—liturgically celebrated, lived out in community, and focused on mission—incorporating all three streams of God's expression in the church. Healing and wholeness happen when the people of God are invited to dip into the divergent streams, and find the joy in tapping the source of the river. The guardian traditions and the sectarian movements that renew the church from time to time, can flow together into one mighty river. Since no stream alone contains the healing waters, joy comes from the living waters found at the source and end of all three. "There is a river whose streams make glad the city of God!"

After two thousand years of church history, denominationalism has run its course. The third millennium demands a new ecumenism. Today's average congregant is postdenominational and doctrinally eclectic. Christians, if they choose to join a local church at all, are no longer exclusively loyal to one particular denomination, but claim multiple religious affiliations and identities. They may be a liberal Methodist on Sunday morning, but attend a PromiseKeepers Bible study on Wednesday night. They may be a Pentecostal Baptist on Wednesday and attend the pan-African divination service on Saturday night. The people of God in the twenty-first century are not content with one stream, but want to cross boundaries, swim in different currents, and find their place of ministry in the broader Body of Christ. *TheNextChurch,* I predict, will be denominationally eclectic, theologically combinative, and liturgically blended. Its priests, clergy and lay, will need to avoid simple and shallow denominationalism and learn to swim in all three streams. Congregational members will want to recognize the guardian streams in the broader church. Most important, the priesthood of believers will need to envision and experience the river of God at is source. Thus a new ordering of the ministry of the faithful is required for a new millennium.

171

If the source of the river is one, and if the divergent tributaries of church traditions are intended to fulfill their distinctive purposes and then merge as one, then the *TheNext-Church* should look more like a return to the source—three streams flowing into one river—than one river branching into three. To return to the source is to overcome denominational divisions and affirm the "one, holy, catholic and apostolic church."

If *TheNextChurch* is a blended, combinative, conjunctive fellowship where all three streams are evident, some people will get a bit uncomfortable trying to affirm and swim in all the steams. Self-identified Protestants get a little uptight if too many gifts are manifest; charismatics are not comfortable with too much formality. And Catholics get upset when the Eucharist is left out of worship. But joy and wholeness come through a balance of the traditions that have been anointed by God in two thousand years of church history. A *"one river, three streams"* church may not grow the fastest, according to the homogenous church growth model, but I am convinced it is a more biblical model, and more reflective of the ongoing revelation of what God is doing in the world. And the Lord will continue to add daily to the faithful church those who are *being* saved (Acts 2:47).

I feel my own contribution to the river vision is in exploring through practice and reflection how each stream can organize ministry and mobilize the people of God. Reflecting on the ecclesial meaning of the three streams, I have gleaned some helpful generalities: The charismatic emphasis on the unity of the Spirit primarily expresses itself in intimate **community.** The Catholic emphasis on the transcendence and majesty of God expresses itself in formal **worship.** And the Protestant emphasis on the work of Christ is best expressed in social **mission.** Therefore, in the interest of understanding how the river of God as a unifier brings healing and wholeness to broken lives, I have identified the three constitutive streams as **community, worship, and mission** in the life of the church (see chart below).

The Threefold Ministry of the Baptized

"And there are three that bear witness in earth, the Spirit, and the water, and the blood: and these three agree in one." (1 John 5:8 KJV)

STREAM	IMAGE	TRADITION	EXPRESSION
COMMUNITY	SPIRIT	CHARISMATIC	PASTORAL Discipleship Cells/groups Celebration Care
MISSION	WATER	PROTESTANT	PROPHETIC Proclamation Teaching Outreach Social justice
WORSHIP	BLOOD	CATHOLIC	PRIESTLY Eucharist Liturgy Musicality Spirituality

The Stream Called Community

What can heal alienation and despair? A stream of belonging and support flowing to those who feel unloved and unwanted. In community there are ingredients for healing the most damaged emotions. Only in community can these disciplines be practiced: *bearing one another's burdens* (Galatians 6:2), *speaking the truth in love* (Ephesians 4:15), *confronting idleness, encouraging timidity and strengthening weakness* (1 Thessalonians 5:14), *confessing faults one to another* (James 5:16a), and *praying for one another that you may be healed* (James 5:16b).

The strength to live the Christian life comes through the structures of community life—small groups organized for fellowship, accountability, confession, and support. In Acts we read how the first Christians met daily in one another's homes, and how they "devoted themselves to the apostles'

173

teaching and to the fellowship, to the breaking of bread and to prayer." We are thrilled about the "wonders and miraculous signs . . . done by the apostles." We are struck by how the early believers "were together and had everything in common." And we are challenged by their example of radical stewardship: "Selling their possessions and goods, they gave to anyone as he had need" (Acts 2:42-45).

It is easy to idealize community life, based on our perception of the early church in Jerusalem during the first few years after Pentecost. It only takes a quick look at Paul's epistles to young church communities to lose the idealism. They, too, had conflicts and besetting sins as they learned to love God and live with one another. Apparently, the communal practice of the early church in Jerusalem did not last the century.

I have witnessed radical stewardship and the common life in monasteries that have a "community purse" and practice the traditional disciplines of simplicity, chastity, and obedience. But seldom do such intensive communities work outside of monastic orders. A more practical approach, I believe, is the informal order of the *laos* of God: Christians living together or in close proximity, gathering regularly for prayer and support, managing their own finances as faithful stewards, and giving freely to the needs of others. Common meals, shared activities, and accountability are essential for "life together"—the meaning of community. Without the benefits of community, Christianity is a solo experience that leaves one unconnected to the whole. The one who embraces community finds a new identity and a place of belonging. In the process, one overcomes the fear of rejection, replaces selfishness with sharing; the rough edges of one's personality are rubbed smooth with the oil of gladness, and one's bitterness is refreshed by the springs of love. Together we find the strength to be Christ's body in the world.

After graduating from seminary and spending thirty days in preparation for urban ministry in a rural Trappist monastery, I was eager to start a prophetic Christian community in the city. I desired to form a "priesthood of believers" who were contemplative in spiritual practice, charismatic in community life, eucharistic in worship, and active in social ministry. Golden Gate Community was a vision fulfilled in the Haight-Ashbury neighborhood of San Francisco. During our first year in the city (1981–82), five of us came together and committed ourselves to morning and evening liturgical prayers, common meals, and service to the poor. The community house we purchased (a four-story, fourteen-room Victorian near the Park) afforded us time and space to be together and to learn the lessons of the common life.

During our second year, as the original members dispersed and others came to be associated with the community, we redefined what we were committed to becoming: *"people on a similar path, sharing a common purpose and lifestyle, living together or in close proximity so as to be in daily contact, in order to build relationships for the sake of mission."* As people moved into and out of the community house and community relationships, we learned that community is not paradise. It is hard work for a diverse group of individuals to become a family unit, agree on division of labor and shared leadership, work together without strife and envy for a common good, and share the common life. But through faith and perseverance, healing waters can be found in a season of intentional and intensive community.

By the third year, Golden Gate Community had become a viable house-church, its members not as radical perhaps as were the early believers in Jerusalem, but devoted to Christ and committed to one another so as to exemplify God's love in our neighborhood. We were willing to be judged by a biblical standard of *orthocardia*: "All . . . will know that you are my disciples, if you love one another" (John 13:35 NIV).

The charismatic stream—with its emphasis on cell groups of accountability, *koinonia* (fellowship), intimate spiritual relationships in the Body of Christ, spiritual gifts, and divine healing—is the guardian tradition of community life. However, the community stream has been enriched by the radical Protestant practice of the priesthood of all believers and egalitarian relationships in the Body of Christ. The Church of the Saviour in Washington, D.C., for example, is a Protestant model of intentional community, requiring *solidarity* in identity, *mutuality* in relationships, *authenticity* in expression, and commitment to the fellowship as the essential ingredients of a healing community.

According to Elizabeth O'Connor, when two or more find themselves on a similar path, bonds of *solidarity* can be formed. A "similar path" means to share a common cause, concern, or vision for ministry. What is shared in common provides the basis for *mutuality*—equality in the give and take of relationships. Egalitarian communities have no need of clergy and laity distinctions, for all are priests and ministers who serve one another for the common good.

Married to solidarity and mutuality are *authenticity* and *commitment*. *Authenticity*, says O'Connor, means that when all is said and done the gift we have to give is to be our real selves with one another. "We dip into our own lives and offer what we find there."[7] *Commitment* in community means to make a willful choice not to abandon the group when times are hard. As O'Connor explains: "Certainly within our own small communities we must have a lasting commitment to one another, so that each knows that the other is not going to pull out of the relationship when the going gets rough."[8] Authenticity and commitment build relationships that mirror our relationship with God. "Community happens," says O'Connor, "when we dare to be naked not only in the presence of God but in the presence of each other, dare to let others see our weaknesses and our strengths, dare to let another hold us accountable."[9]

Devotion to God and commitment to one another, in an environment where solidarity, mutuality, and authenticity are present, tap into the healing stream of community. "How good and pleasant it is when brothers [and sisters] live together in unity!" sings the psalmist about the blessings of community life:

> It is like precious oil poured on the head,
>> running down on the beard,
> running down on Aaron's beard,
>> down upon the collar of his robes.
> It is as if the dew of Hermon
>> were falling on Mount Zion.
> For there the LORD bestows his blessing,
>> even life forevermore. (Psalm 133 NIV)

The Stream Called Worship

After three years of struggling with issues of solidarity, mutuality, authenticity, and commitment, Golden Gate Community was ready for a new challenge. It was during our third year as a community that we discovered the importance of corporate praise and worship. "Let us not give up meeting together," we reminded ourselves, "but let us encourage one another" in word, sacrament and song (Hebrews 10:25 NIV).

There is a therapeutic quality in worship. We are by nature or nurture self-oriented and individualistic. To worship means to let go and let God in. To worship is to give credit to God as that Power greater than ourselves. Praise lifts the heart and lets it sing. The healing waters of worship are like pounding ocean waves lifting up their crests to God:

> The seas have lifted up, O LORD,
>> the seas have lifted up their voice;
>> the seas have lifted up their pounding waves.
> Mightier than the thunder of the great waters,
>> mightier than the breakers of the sea—
>> the LORD on high is mighty. (Psalm 93:3-4 NIV)

The Orthodox-Catholic-Episcopal stream is the guardian tradition of eucharistic worship. The Divine Liturgy, at least for me, is where worship connects heaven and earth in the beauty of holiness and adoration (Revelation 4). In eucharistic worship, praise to God is often chanted and the *Sanctus* sung from the heart. The sacraments embody that to which they point. Weekly Communion helps rejuvenate body, soul, and spirit. Though a designated "official" priest *re-presents* Christ at table, all who participate in the Supper are priests unto the Lord. Neither Protestant nor charismatic worship approaches the Great Thanksgiving, the Mystery of Faith and transcendent glory as well as the Catholic/Orthodox stream.

However, the liturgical stream requires renewal from time to time. Charismatics, more than Protestants, serve to renew and enhance the worship stream. Charismatic Episcopal worship, for example, has for many been liberating and therapeutic in the way traditional liturgy is blended with contemporary praise and participation. Former Catholics often find in charismatic and Protestant worship something they missed in their own tradition. What is important in the stream of worship is not the liturgical style but the spiritual function and effect. True worshipers, whether at the Samaritan mountain, in the Jewish Temple, or in the early Christian house-church, approach the Living God "in spirit and in truth" (John 4:24).

Worship is the "action that brings the Christ-event into the experience of the community gathered in the name of Jesus," Robert Webber reminds us in his book on liturgical worship for evangelical Protestants. It is participatory prayer and drama.[10] In the *Pastoral Greeting* ("The Lord be with you"), the people respond ("And also with you"). During the *Profession of Faith,* the people of God join in reciting the Apostles' Creed, reminding ourselves of what we believe about God. During the *Prayers of the People,* all intentions are affirmed ("Lord, hear our prayer"). During the *Passing of the Peace,* people embrace one another with a kiss, hug, or handshake, breaking down barriers that divide. In the *Lord's Prayer,* or in songs sung in preparation to receive the *Lord's Supper,* people often feel free to lift up their hands in praise, worshiping God both with their hearts and their bodies. During *Holy Communion,* people come forward to kneel and receive the healing sacrament. "Here a hand from the hidden country touches not only my soul but my body," writes C. S. Lewis.[11] Having experienced a taste of things to come, worshipers are blessed with a *Benediction* and sent back into the world as priests and ministers of the apostolic tradition.

Worship need not be formal, but whether liturgical or free form, it should lift the heart, give God glory, and transform the participant. Forms and styles of worship vary, but the spiritual function and effect remains the same. Praise and worship directed toward God as the audience not only blesses God but us. In fact, worship done well is probably more for our benefit than God's. While God is glorified when we worship truly, we ourselves are spiritually renewed in the process. The community gathers in worship to find the strength to go back out into the world to make a difference, having bathed for a moment in a healing stream.

The Stream Called Mission

The church *(ecclesia)* literally means the "called out ones"—called out of the world and into community for the sake of worship and mission in the world. The dynamic is like a three-legged stool—one leg cannot stand without the support from the others. The structure is like a triangle— without the foundation of community life, expressing itself upward in worship and outward in mission, the whole thing would crumble.

179

Just as healing is to be found in the inward journey of community and the upward journey of worship, there is a healing journey to be traveled in helping others. People often feel victimized and helpless. "Why me, Lord?" is the prayer of someone who needs the healing presence and empowerment of another called to ministry. One can forget about one's own problems as one seeks to meet the needs of others. There is no time to wallow in self-pity when there is a whole world to serve and save. To paraphrase Oral Roberts, an unlikely prophet in the Protestant stream: *Sow seeds of compassion in the soil of someone else's need and expect God to meet your needs as well.* Saint Francis said it best: "It is in giving that we receive."

The Protestant churches, with their emphasis on social reform, outreach ministry, and community service, form the guardian tradition of the mission stream. However, Catholic workers and charismatic missionaries witness to the need for this stream to be renewed from time to time. Mother Teresa, more than any other modern Catholic activist, embodies the truth of Jesus' challenge in Matthew 25: "Whatever you did for one of the least of these brothers of mine, you did for me" (v. 40 NIV). Charismatics, too, renew the mission stream. Note, for example, how many soup kitchens, neighborhood shelters, drug rehabilitation programs, and mentoring ministries in the city are staffed by charismatics and Pentecostals. In contrast, Protestant churches today tend to sponsor and finance social service agencies that help at-risk clients, rather than involving their members in direct, hands-on services to the poor and oppressed in Jesus' name. The mission stream needs the renewal efforts of individuals and communities who give "a cup of water in my name" (Mark 9:41 NIV).

I started Golden Gate Community in 1981 as a prophetic Christian community focused on the needs of poor and homeless persons in Haight-Ashbury. Before the end of the second year, we had become a worshiping community of thirty persons celebrating the Eucharist and agape weekly in a house-church. During our third year, several neighborhood ministries had begun, including: the Oak Street House for people in transition, the Haight-Ashbury Soup Kitchen and the Hamilton Family Shelter. Before our sixth anniversary, Golden Gate Community had started a job development program and the Bridge for Kids: a ministry to children with HIV and their families. Each of these ministries was staffed by church members and volunteers who felt ownership of the church and its neighborhood mission. In time Golden Gate Community church and mission split into two separate organizations, each focused on a different stream. While the church prioritized worship and community life, the mission specialized in community development and transitional housing. The church outgrew the house community and became a midsize city church. The mission became a successful social service agency. Only together, however, could Golden Gate Community church and mission become a "three streams, one river" revelation of God in the world.[12]

There is a river whose three healing streams make whole the people of God: In community life, we express our commitment to the Body of Christ. In worship of God, we increase our corporate joy. In mission we channel the healing waters we have found to the needs of others. Cross-pollination, or rather, believers swimming in the cross-currents of all the streams, renews the church and brings health and wholeness to individual members. As these streams flow together, the river mobilizes clergy and laity to swim as one.

Visualizing a One River Church

"Three streams, one river"—incorporating the best of the Catholic, Protestant, and charismatic guardian traditions—makes glad the city and brings balance to the community of faith. The challenge is to find a way to activate these expressions in the life of the church and allow the springs of healing water to flow from God's heart to every human heart. Anthony Campolo suggests such a structure, though a practicing model is harder to find. Campolo's ideal church comes in the form of a visionary dream:

> We need a Church that will do what God created it to do . . . that is willing to divest itself of wealth, power and prestige for the sake of the poor and distraught. We need a Church which will imitate its Founder and adopt the role of the Suffering Servant. . . .
>
> I have a dream. I long for a Church organized in small cellular units of four or five members. I see each of these groups committed to some mission in the world. . . . There would be a pastor, but his [or her] job would be far different from that of the typical clergy. The pastor would be a resource person for these groups. He [or she] would help them understand what the Bible has to say about what they are trying to accomplish.
>
> The laity would realize their true potential through the action of these groups. Laypeople would no longer be second-class Christians whose only purpose is to support the clergy in their ministry. Instead, the laity would be viewed as the real ministers of the Gospel, and the clergy would be viewed as persons called to equip these saints to fulfill their calling (Eph 4:11-12).
>
> Each Sunday these groups would join together for corporate worship. The worship services would be different from what is typical in most churches. Each group would tell what it was doing, what God had accomplished through its efforts and how persons had been evangelized through its message. As each report was given, other groups would sing for joy because of what God was doing. They would be filled with praise for the One who is directing the revolution. They would sing of the kingdom which was breaking loose in history.[13]

Campolo envisions a one-river church of clergy and laity, organized in small cells or mission groups, coming together for corporate worship, and being inspired to go back out into the world to build the Kingdom. This is only a dream, he admits. "But it is a dream that can become a reality."[14] My dream is for *TheNextChurch* to be unified and activated in community, worship, and mission in the world; each stream serving to mobilize called and gifted ministers around its particular emphasis; each uniquely offering its healing waters to those who swim in its current; together forming one river of wholeness and peace.

God's dream is for the river of life—envisioned by Ezekiel, Isaiah, and John—to make glad the city. On that great day when all the world shall feast, the curse will be lifted. "The throne of God and of the Lamb will be in the city. . . . There will be no more night," for the Lord will shine. "And they will reign for ever and ever" (Revelation 22:3-5). On that day, the "wolf will live with the lamb, the leopard will lie down with the goat, the calf and the lion and the yearling together; and a little child will lead them. . . . They will neither harm nor destroy on all my holy mountain, for the earth will be full of the knowledge of the LORD as the waters cover the sea" (Isaiah 11:6, 9).

Until that day when God's dream is realized on earth as it is in heaven, the church is called to witness to God's kingdom here and now, and to work toward the fulfillment of the vision in the age to come.

Let the Healing Waters Flow

The question that began this chapter serves to end this volume: How should ministerial leadership (clergy) move the people of God (laity) from the baptismal font into the full flow of ministry in the church and mission in the world? My hope and vision: May *TheNextChurch* become a "three streams, one river" church of called, gifted, equipped, and mobilized ministers of God. It we wish, then let those called to the worship stream be named "clergy," and those called

183

to the community stream, "lay ministers"; and those called to the mission stream, "deacons." Better yet, simply abolish both the order of the clergy and the laity in favor of a new ordering of the priesthood of believers around the three streams in the one river of God. Let the same biblical psalm that inspired Martin Luther to compose "A Mighty Fortress Is Our God" as the foundation of the Protestant Reformation now serve as a postmodern chant (with accompanying hymns and spiritual songs) in the New Reformation of the Laity:

> God is our refuge and strength,
>   an ever-present help in trouble.
> Therefore we will not fear, though the earth give way
>   and the mountains fall into the heart of the sea,
> though its waters roar and foam
>   and the mountains quake with their surging.
> There is a river whose streams make glad the city of God,
>   the holy place where the Most High dwells.
> God is within her, she will not fall. . . .
> The LORD Almighty is with us;
>   the God of Jacob is our fortress. (Psalm 46:1-5, 7)

NOTES

Foreword

1. Emerito P. Napil, *Jesus' Strategy for Social Transformation* (Nashville: Abingdon, 1999), 214.
2. Jurgen Moltmann, *The Church in the Power of the Holy Spirit* (London: SCM, 1977), 10.

Introduction

1. D. Elton Trueblood, *The Essence of Spiritual Religion* (New York: Harper & Brothers, 1936), pp. 135-36.
2. Lyle E. Schaller, *The New Reformation: Tomorrow Arrived Yesterday* (Nashville: Abingdon, 1996); and *Discontinuity and Hope: Radical Change and the Path to the Future* (Nashville: Abingdon, 1999).
3. Leonard I. Sweet, *SoulTsunami* (Grand Rapids: Zondervan, 1999).
4. Trueblood, *The Essence of Spiritual Religion*, p. 136.
5. *TheNextChurch*—a term and concept that has been used in one form or another by several leadership development and church consultation groups to describe the emerging church of the twenty-first century. I employ the phrase in its conjunctive form to emphasize that *TheNext-Church* will be denominationally eclectic and theologically combinative of the three traditional streams that produced it, namely: Catholic, Protestant, and Pentecostal in content, style, and spirit. See Chapter Seven "Three Streams, One River" in this volume.
6. Leonard Sweet, *Aquachurch* (Loveland, Colo.: Group Publishing Inc., 1999).

Chapter 1

1. Attributed to Daniel Boorstin by David Olshine in a sermon delivered on September 1, 1990, at First United Methodist Church in Tulsa, Oklahoma.
2. Paul Yonggi Cho, *Successful Home Groups* (South Plainfield, N.J.: Bridge Publishing Inc., 1978).
3. A helpful resource for creating a servant church is Robert Greenleaf's

Servant Leadership: A Journey into the Nature of Legitimate Power and Greatness (New York: Paulist, 1983).

Chapter 2

1. D. Elton Trueblood, *The Essence of Spiritual Religion* (New York: Harper & Brothers, 1936), p. 137.

2. R. Paul Stevens and Phil Collins, *The Equipping Pastor: A Systems Approach to Congregational Leadership* (Bethesda, Md.: Alban Institute, 1993), p. 138.

3. Cyril C. Richardson, trans. and ed., *Early Christian Fathers,* Library of Christian Classics, vol. 1 (Philadelphia: Westminster, 1953), p. 62.

4. George Huntston Williams, "The Ancient Church, AD 30–313," in *The Layman in Christian History,* ed. Stephen Charles Neill and Hans-Ruedi Weber (Philadelphia: Westminster, 1963), p. 30.

5. Alexandre Faivre, *The Emergence of the Laity in the Early Church,* trans. David Smith (New York: Paulist, 1990), p. 209.

6. Ibid., p. 5.

7. *Dialogue with Trypho,* 116, in *Ante-Nicene Christian Library,* vol. II: Justin Martyr and Athenagoras (Edinburgh: T&T. Clark, 1867), pp. 245-46.

8. Williams, "The Ancient Church, AD 30-313," p. 31.

9. Cyril Eastwood, *The Priesthood of All Believers: An Examination of the Doctrine from the Reformation to the Present Day* (Minneapolis: Augsburg, 1962), p. xi.

10. Paul Bradshaw, *Liturgical Presidency in the Early Church,* Grove Liturgical Study No. 36 (Bramcote, England: Grove Books, 1983), p. 9.

11. L. William Countryman, *Living on the Border of the Holy: Renewing the Priesthood of All* (Harrisburg, Pa.: Morehouse, 1999), p. 130.

12. Ibid., p. 131.

13. Bradshaw, *Liturgical Presidency in the Early Church,* p. 10.

14. Faivre, *The Emergence of the Laity in the Early Church,* p. 211.

15. Eastwood, *The Priesthood of All Believers,* p. xii.

16. Faivre, *The Emergence of the Laity in the Early Church,* p. 212.

17. E. Gordon Rupp, "The Age of the Reformation 1500–1648," in *The Layman in Christian History,* ed. Stephen Charles Neill and Hans-Ruedi Weber (Philadelphia: Westminster, 1963), p. 139.

18. Eastwood, *The Priesthood of All Believers,* p. 20.

19. Ibid., p. 6.

20. Countryman, *Living on the Border of the Holy,* p. 112.

21. Ibid., p. 86.

22. Quoted in *Shopping for Faith: American Religion in the New Millennium,* Richard Cimino and Don Lattin (San Francisco: Jossey-Bass, 1998), p. 84.

Chapter 3

1. Gilbert Bilezikian, Introduction to *Group Life: Pursuing Spiritual Transformation,* by John Ortberg, Laurie Pederson, and Judson Poling (South Barrington, Ill.: Willow Creek Community Church, 1998), p. 7.

2. John Ortberg, "A Call for Endurance," audiocassette (South Barrington, Ill.: Willow Creek Community Church, April 21, 1999).

3. Mary Pipher, *Another Country: Navigating the Emotional Terrain of Our Elders* (New York: Riverhead, 1999), p. 68.

4. Dietrich Bonhoeffer, *Life Together,* trans. John W. Doberstein (New York: Harper & Row, 1954).

5. Methodist societies were large groups, sometimes several hundred people, who met weekly for teaching and worship. Band meetings were subsets of the society, small clusters of five to ten (grouped according to gender, age, and marital status), that met in homes for intensive times of accountability and fellowship. Class meetings, also subsets of the society, had a similar purpose to band meetings, but were run somewhat differently and organized geographically rather than by gender, age, and marital status. Today's Wesleyan small-group model takes the form of Covenant Discipleship Groups in The United Methodist Church. David Lowes Watson's *Accountable Discipleship: Handbook for Covenant Discipleship Groups in the Congregation* presents this model in depth.

6. David S. Hunsicker, "John Wesley: Father of Today's Small Group Concept?" *Wesleyan Theological Journal* 31 (spring 1996).

7. Bill Donahue, "Growing Small: A Look at Creating and Maintaining Life-Changing Small Groups," *WCA News* 6, no. 6 (November/December 1998), p. 3.

8. Jarrett Pautz, interview with the author (April 22, 1999).

9. Bill Donahue, interview with the author (March 17, 1999). Please note that unless otherwise stated, all material attributed to Bill Donahue is taken from this interview.

10. Founded in 1992, the Willow Creek Association (WCA) is an international organization with five thousand members from more than eighty denominations in eighteen countries. In addition to publishing a wide range of resources, the WCA conducts international conferences on church leadership, the arts, evangelism, small groups, youth ministry, and children's ministry. In 1999 more than sixty thousand attended conferences offered by the WCA.

11. Carl F. George, *Prepare Your Church for the Future* (Grand Rapids: Fleming H. Revell, 1991), p. 51.

12. Ibid., pp. 51-52.

13. Donahue, "Growing Small: A Look at Creating and Maintaining Life-changing Small Groups," pp. 3-4.

14. Bill Donahue, *Leading Life-Changing Small Groups* (Grand Rapids: Zondervan, 1996), p. 145.

15. Carl George, *Prepare Your Church for the Future,* p. 99.

16. Donahue, "Growing Small: A Look at Creating and Maintaining Life-changing Small Groups," p. 4.

17. The Fellowship of Christian Athletes remains a thriving ministry on high school and college campuses throughout the United States. Its stated mission is to "present Jesus Christ to athletes and coaches and all whom they influence with the challenge of receiving Jesus Christ as Savior

and Lord, and the adventure of receiving Jesus Christ as Savior and Lord, serving him in their relationships and in the fellowship of the Church." FCA's goal is to have a presence on every school campus in America. In 1999, there were more than seventy-four hundred groups with an estimated five hundred thousand students involved.

18. Don McClanen, interview with the author (May 3, 1999).

19. Mary Crosby, interview with the author (April 29, 1999).

20. Gordon Crosby, *Handbook for Mission Groups* (Waco, Tex.: Word, 1975), p. 54

21. Lisa Hughey, interview with the author (April 29, 1999).

22. Van Pewthers, interview with the author (April 30, 1999).

23. Richard Cimino and Don Lattin, *Shopping for Faith: American Religion in the New Millennium* (San Francisco: Jossey-Bass, 1998), pp. 95-96.

24. The name *First Fruits* was changed to *Equipping the Saints* in 1987, and changed again in 1997 to *Voice of the Vineyard,* its current title.

25. In 1999, there were 449 Vineyard congregations in the United States and 370 international congregations.

26. "RENOVARÉ: Bringing the Church to the Churches," booklet, (Englewood, Col.: RENOVARÉ, Inc., undated), inside cover.

27. Valerie Hess, interview with the author (March 21, 1999).

28. See Richard J. Foster, *Streams of Living Water* (San Francisco: HarperSanFrancisco, 1998).

29. Richard J. Foster, *A Personal Message from Richard J. Foster and Interview of Board Members,* audiocassette (Englewood, Col.: RENOVARÉ, Inc.).

30. Ibid.

31. Ibid.

32. Ibid.

33. Ibid.

34. "RENOVARÉ: Bringing the Church to the Churches," booklet (Englewood, Col.: RENOVARÉ:, Inc., undated), pp. 2-3.

35. James Bryan Smith et al., *A Spiritual Formation Workbook: Small Group Resources for Nurturing Christian Growth,* rev. ed. (San Francisco: HarperSanFrancisco, 1999), p. 99.

36. In 1991 when *A Spiritual Formation Workbook* was first published, the RENOVARÉ model outlined five rather than six traditions. The revised edition, published in 1999, includes the sixth tradition.

37. Dallas Willard, *A Personal Message from Richard J. Foster and Interview of Board Members.*

38. "RENOVARÉ: Bringing the Church to the Churches," p. 5.

39. Ibid.

40. James Bryan Smith, *A Personal Message from Richard J. Foster and the Interview of Board Members.*

41. Richard J. Foster, *A Personal Message from Richard J. Foster and Interview of Board Members.*

42. Parker J. Palmer, "The Clearness Committee: A Way of Discernment," *Weavings* (July/August 1988), p. 38.

43. Beth Burbank, interview with the author (March 24, 1999).
44. Patricia Loring, "Spiritual Discernment: The Context and Goal of Clearness Committees," Pendle Hill Pamphlet 305, (Wallingford, Pa.: Pendle Hill Publications, 1992), p. 4.
45. Ibid., p. 21.
46. Parker J. Palmer, *The Courage to Teach: Exploring the Inner Landscape of a Teacher's Life* (San Francisco: Jossey-Bass, 1998), p. 151.
47. Ibid., p. 153.
48. Ibid.
49. Parker J. Palmer, "The Clearness Committee: A Way of Discernment," p. 39.
50. Parker J. Palmer, *The Courage to Teach,* p. 155.
51. Ibid.
52. Ibid.
53. C. S. Lewis, *The Great Divorce* (New York: MacMillan, 1946), p. 65.
54. C. S. Lewis, *The Problem of Pain* (New York: MacMillan, 1962), pp. 127-28.

Chapter 4

1. Christ United Methodist Church of Bethel Park, Pennsylvania, is a congregation of more than three thousand members ten minutes south of downtown Pittsburgh.
2. See my treatment of this understanding and especially of the book of Ephesians as a "manual" for bringing the church into being for growing a body of believers, in my book *Body Building* (Abingdon, 1996).
3. From Christ United Methodist Church's vision statement.
4. See my *Body Building,* p. 16.
5. See my *Body Building,* chapter 3, note 1.
6. These positions currently include: two ordained deacons: one for music and one for youth; five program staff or administrative directors: (1) children's ministries, (2) church growth and communication, (3) Christian formation and program, (4) administration and stewardship, (5) financial operations; four administrative assistants: (1) senior administrative assistant/music associate, (2) program secretary, (3) worship secretary, and (4) membership secretary; finally, an organist/director of worship life and a facilities manager.
7. Our policy is to offer lay staff positions at a salary that is competitive with the nonprofit sector in southwest Pennsylvania. A fully licensed CPA in the for-profit sector of the economy could easily start at more than twice what we would be able to pay.
8. The marvelous image of the "servant leader" and the term "first among equals" initially came to my awareness in the writings of Robert Greenleaf, a Quaker lecturer and writer. Most significant was his book entitled *Servant Leadership* published in 1983.
9. See Chapter Two in this volume for Professor Moy's treatment of the rise and fall of lay ministry in church history.
10. I find no consistent list of what are considered *the* viable, authen-

tic spiritual gifts in Scripture or in Christian literature. In all probability, Paul and others never intended to provide an exhaustive list. He simply wanted the principle to be operative and evident in the life of the church.

11. This refers to the recent and widely used *Disciple Bible Study* used throughout The United Methodist Church and within other denominations.

12. The Meyers-Briggs Type Indicator is usually administered by a licensed and trained leader. The results indicate whether an individual is more extroverted or introverted, more intuitive or sensing, more thinking or feeling, or more perceptive or judging in his or her preferred style. This tool is often administered to assist a multiple-person staff in understanding and responding to one another in a more caring, informed fashion. For more reading on this particular inventory, see *Please Understand Me: Character and Temperament Types* by David Keirsey and Marilyn Bates (Del Mar, Calif.: Prometheus Nemesis Book Co., 1984).

13. The consultants are persons who have completed the spiritual gifts assessment class, who have demonstrated a desire to volunteer in this task. They are always lay members of the congregation who are trained for this specific purpose. We currently have two persons in this function who are serving ably and enthusiastically.

Chapter 5

1. Stanley J. Grenz, *A Primer on Postmodernism* (Grand Rapids: Eerdmans, 1996), p. 174.

2. The term "seeker-sensitive worship" was coined by Bill Hybels, founding pastor of Willow Creek Community, in the early 1970s. Today, the Willow Creek Association prefers the term "seeker-targeted worship."

3. John Wesley, *The Works of John Wesley,* 3rd ed., Letters, vol. XIII (Grand Rapids: Baker Book House, 1978), pp. 307-8.

4. Leonard Sweet's book, *11 Genetic Gateways to Spiritual Awakening* (Abingdon, 1998) is a helpful resource in the quest to gain a deeper understanding of those "genetic" characteristics that equip United Methodism to face the future in meaningful ways.

5. For an excellent analysis of the characteristics of the postmodern ethos, see Stanley Grenz's book, *A Primer on Postmodernism.*

6. *The Works of John Wesley,* vol. 13, *Letters* (Grand Rapids: Baker Book House, 1978), pp. 307-8.

7. Lee Strobel, *Inside the Mind of Unchurched Harry and Mary* (Grand Rapids: Zondervan, 1993), p. 168.

8. For a detailed description of the heart, mind, and soul of the genuine spiritual seeker, see Lee Strobel's *Inside the Mind of Unchurched Harry and Mary.* Strobel, a former spiritual skeptic, offers keen insight concerning the mind-set of the contemporary unchurched.

9. George G. Hunter III, *Church for the Unchurched* (Nashville: Abingdon, 1996), p. 20.

10. Ibid.

11. Ibid.

12. Leonard Sweet describes this cultural proclivity to individualism as

"cocooning" in his book, *Faithquakes* (Nashville: Abingdon, 1995), pp. 21-26.

13. Lewis H. Lapham, "Punch and Judy," *Harper's*, September 1998, p. 15.

Chapter 6

1. Leonard Sweet, *SoulTsunami* (Grand Rapids: Zondervan, 1999), p. 32.

2. Ian Morrison, *The Second Curve* (New York: Ballantine, 1997), quoted in Price Pritchett, *Mindshift* (Dallas: Pritchett Publishing Co., 1996), p. 27.

3. Leonard Sweet, public lecture, Drew University, September 16, 1997.

4. Visit *http.//da.cihost.com/nextchurch* for resources of the electronification of the church.

5. Visit *www.drew.edu/interneteducation* for online learning options at Drew Theological School.

Chapter 7

1. "Ministry" here means forms of care, support, witness, teaching, and service that members of a congregation provide to one another.

2. "Mission" is service, witness, and justice provided to those outside the congregation.

3. The psalm that inspired Martin Luther to compose "A Mighty Fortress Is Our God" contains a mighty river image to "make glad" the city. The Hebrew phrase translated "make glad" in the King James Version may also be translated "refresh," "bring life and joy," or "make whole" the people of God (Psalm 46:4).

4. A pastoral letter From Richard J. Foster (RENOVARÉ Newsletter, November 1988).

5. Ibid.

6. Richard Foster, *Streams of Living Water* (San Francisco: Harper-SanFrancisco, 1998), p. xv.

7. Elizabeth O'Connor, *Letters to Scattered Pilgrims* (San Francisco: Harper & Row, 1979), p. xv.

8. Ibid., p. 99.

9. Ibid., p. 104.

10. Robert E. Webber, *Worship Old and New: A Biblical, Historical, and Practical Introduction* (Grand Rapids: Zondervan, 1982).

11. C. S. Lewis, *Letters to Malcolm: Chiefly on Prayer* (New York: Harcourt, Brace & World), p. 103.

12. For the story of how the "three-streams, one-river" paradigm was developed and applied at Golden Gate Community in San Francisco, see my *City Streets, City People: A Call to Compassion* (Nashville: Abingdon, 1989).

13. Anthony Campolo, *Ideas for Social Action: A Handbook on Mission and Service for Christian Young People* (Grand Rapids: Zondervan, 1991), pp. 14-16.

14. Ibid., p. 16.

Selected Bibliography on Mobilizing Laity

Compiled by Carl E. Savage

The works cited in this bibliography are selected as representational of what is available in the relatively new field of Mobilizing Laity. They are grouped first according to the paradigm of understanding they represent: Premodern, Modern (General), and Postmodern. Those in the Premodern category are works by authors who were leaders in the ancient church or secondary sources that describe the general ministry of the laity throughout church history. As we rediscover the ancient church, we may find the early church leaders' insights concerning timeless truth may again find applicability in the contemporary context.

Those in the second group, General Resources, are works that build upon the traditional model of church ministry found, for the most part, among Protestant and evangelical churches. This category is further subdivided to follow the outline of the material that is contained in this volume, and features works that may be helpful in developing deeper understanding and programming in the areas of theology of ministry, small groups, team leadership, evangelism, contemporary worship, and missional outreach.

The final group, Postmodern, contains works that attempt to stretch our understanding of lay ministry and the nature of the church. The Future Church may find itself communicating the gospel in new and unique ways that include a reformulated understanding of the role of laity in ministry in the postmodern context. These "postmodern" works emphasize our need to be change leaders in a changing church familiar with the new context that is the third millennial world.

Premodern Resources for Historical Precedents

Augustine. *First Catechetical Instruction.* Translated by J. P. Christopher. Ancient Christian Writers, 2. Westminster, Md.: Newman, 1946.

Bartlett, David L. *Ministry in the New Testament.* Minneapolis: Fortress, 1993.

Bradshaw, Paul. *Liturgical Presidency in the Early Church.* Grove Liturgical Study No. 36. Bramcote, England: Grove Books, 1983.

Branick, Vincent P. *The House Church in the Writings of Paul.* Wilmington, Del.: Michael Glazier, 1988.

Clark, Elizabeth A. *Women in the Early Church.* Wilmington, Del.: Michael Glazier, 1983.

Congar, Yves. *Lay People in the Church.* Westminster, Md.: Newman, 1957.

Cyprian. *Treatises.* Translated by C. Thornton. Library of the Fathers. Oxford: J. H. Parker, 1899.

Cyril of Jerusalem. *The Catechetical Lectures.* Edited by W. Telfer. Library of Christian Classics, 4. London: SCM Press, 1965.

Doohan, Leonard. *The Laity: A Bibliography.* Wilmington, Del.: Michael Glazier, 1987.

———. *The Lay Centered Church: Theology and Spirituality.* Minneapolis: Winston, 1984.

Eastwood, Cyril. *The Priesthood of All Believers: An Examination of the Doctrine from the Reformation to the Present Day.* Minneapolis: Augsburg, 1962.

Faivre, Alexandre. *The Emergence of the Laity in the Early Church.* New York: Paulist, 1990.

———. "The Laity in the First Centuries: Issues Revealed by Historical Research," *Lumen Vitae* 42 (1987): 129-39.

Field, O.S.B., Anne. *From Darkness to Light.* Ann Arbor, Mich.: Servant Books, 1978.

Frend, W.H.C., ed. *The Layman in Christian History.* London: SCM, 1963.

Garrett, James L., Jr. "The Pre-Cyprianic Doctrine of the Priesthood of All Christians." In *Continuity and Discontinuity in Church History,* edited by F.F. Church and T. George. Leiden: Brill, 1979, 45-61.

———. "The Priesthood of All Christians: From Cyprian to John Chrysostom," *Southwestern Journal of Theology* 30 (1988): 22-33.

Grabbe, Lester L. *Priests, Prophets, Diviners, Sages: a Socio-historical Study of Religious Specialists in Ancient Israel.* Valley Forge, Pa.: Trinity Press International, 1995.

Green, Michael. *Evangelism in the Early Church.* Grand Rapids: Eerdmans, 1970.

Neill, Stephen Charles, and Hans-Ruedi Weber. *The Layman in Christian History.* Philadelphia: Westminster, 1963.

Osbourne, Kenan B. *Ministry—Lay Ministry in the Roman Catholic Church: Its History and Theology.* New York: Paulist, 1993.

Pelikan, Jaroslav. *Spirit Versus Structure: Luther and the Institutions of the Church.* New York: Harper & Row, 1968.

Ruether, Rosemary, and Eleanor McLaughlin, ed., *Women of Spirit: Female Leadership in the Jewish and Christian Traditions.* New York: Simon and Schuster, 1998.

Richardson, Cyril C., trans. and ed. *Early Christian Fathers.* Library of Christian Classics, 1. Philadelphia: Westminster, 1953.

Ryan, L. "Patristic Teaching on the Priesthood of the Faithful," *ITQ* 29 (1962): 25-51.

Snyder, Howard A. *The Radical Wesley and Patterns for Church Renewal.* Downers Grove, Ill.: InterVarsity Press, 1980.

Volz, Carl A. *Pastoral Life and Practice in the Early Church.* Minneapolis: Augsburg, 1990.

Watson, David Lowes. *The Early Methodist Class Meeting: Its Origin and Significance.* Nashville: Discipleship Resources, 1987.

General Resources for a Changing Church

Priesthood of All Believers

Anderson, James D., and Ezra Earl Jones. *The Management of Ministry.* San Francisco: Harper & Row, 1978.

Anderson, Leith. *A Church for the 21ST Century.* Minneapolis: Bethany House, 1992.

Anderson, Ray. *Ministry on the Fireline: A Practical Theology for an Empowered Church.* Downer's Grove, Ill.: InterVarsity Press, 1993.

Barna, George. *The Second Coming of the Church.* Nashville: Word, 1998.

Beard, Margaret L., and Roger W. Comstock, ed. *All Are Chosen: Stories of Lay Ministry and Leadership.* Boston: Skinner House Books, 1998.

Beckham, William A. *The Second Reformation: Reshaping the Church for the 21ST Century.* Houston: Touch Publications, 1995.

Braaten, Carl. *The Apostolic Imperative.* Minneapolis: Augsburg, 1985.

Cooper, Norman P. *Collaborative Ministry: Communion, Contention, Commitment.* New York: Paulist, 1993.

Costa, Donna M. *The Ministry of God's People.* Nashville: Discipleship Resources, 1991.

Countryman, L. William. *Living on the Border of the Holy: Renewing the Priesthood of All.* Harrisburg, Pa.: Morehouse, 1999.

Fulenwider, Ray. *The Servant-Driven Church: Releasing Every Member for Ministry.* Joplin, Mo.: College Press, 1998.

Greenleaf, Robert K. *Seeker and Servant: Reflections on Religious Leadership.* Edited by Anne T. Fraker and Larry C. Spears. San Francisco: Jossey-Bass, 1996.

————. *Servant Leadership: A Journey into the Nature of Legitimate Power and Greatness*. New York: Paulist, 1977.

Hall, Eddy, and Gary Morsch. *The Lay Ministry Revolution: How You Can Join*. Grand Rapids: Baker Book House, 1995.

Jones, Ezra Earl, and James D. Anderson. *The Management of Ministry: Building Leadership in a Changing World*. Nashville: Discipleship Resources, 1998.

Karmires, Ioannes N., and Evie Marie Zachariades-Holmberg. *The Status and Ministry of the Laity in the Orthodox Church*. Brookline, Mass.: Holy Cross Orthodox Press, 1992.

Malphurs, Aubrey. *Pouring New Wine Into Old Wineskins: How to Change a Church Without Destroying It*. Grand Rapids: Baker Book House, 1993.

Mead, Loren. *The Once and Future Church*. Washington, D.C.: The Alban Institute, 1991.

————. *Transforming Congregations for the Future*. New York: The Alban Institute, 1994.

Miller, Donald. *Reinventing American Protestantism*. Berkeley: University of California Press, 1997.

Ogden, Greg. *The New Reformation: Returning the Ministry to the People of God*. Grand Rapids: Zondervan, 1990.

Schaller, Lyle E. *Discontinuity and Hope: Radical Change and the Path to the Future*. Nashville: Abingdon, 1999.

————. *The New Reformation: Tomorrow Arrived Yesterday*. Nashville: Abingdon, 1996.

Wink, Walter. *Unmasking the Powers*. Philadelphia: Fortress, 1986.

Zabriske, Stewart C. *Total Ministry: Reclaiming the Ministry of All God's People*. Washington, D.C.: The Alban Institute, 1995.

Small Groups

Bandy, Thomas. *Kicking Habits: Welcome Relief for Addicted Churches*. Nashville: Abingdon, 1997.

Bellah, Robert, et al. *Habits of the Heart: Individualism and Commitment in American Life*. Los Angeles: University of California Press, 1996.

Cho, Paul Yonggi. *Successful Home Cell Groups*. South Plainfield, N.J.: Bridge Publishing, 1978.

Cosby, Gordon. *Handbook for Mission Groups*. Waco, TX: Word, 1975.

Donahue, Bill. *Leading Life-Changing Small Groups*. Grand Rapids: Zondervan, 1996.

————. *The Willow Creek Guide to Life-changing Small Groups*. Grand Rapids: Zondervan, 1994.

George, Carl F. *Prepare Your Church for the Future*. Grand Rapids: Revell, 1992.

Hestenes, Roberta. *Turning Committees into Communities*. Colorado Springs, Col.: NavPress, 1991.

Ortberg, John, Laurie Pederson, and Judson Polling. *Group Life: Pursuing Spiritual Transformation*. South Barrington, Ill.: Willow Creek Community Church, 1998.

Palmer, Parker. *The Courage to Teach: Exploring the Inner Landscape of a Teacher's Life*. San Francisco: Jossey-Bass, 1998.

Pipher, Mary. *Another Country: Navigating the Emotional Terrain of Our Elders.* New York: Riverhead, 1999.

Smith, James Bryan. *A Spiritual Formation Workbook: Small Groups for Nurturing Christian Growth.* San Francisco: HarperSanFrancisco, 1991.

Steinke, Peter L. *How Your Church Family Works.* New York: The Alban Institute, 1993.

Watson, David Lowe. *Accountable Discipleship: Handbook for Covenant Discipleship Groups in the Congregation.* Nashville: Discipleship Resources, 1984.

Team Building

Anderson, Ray Sherman. *The Soul of Ministry: Forming Leaders for God's People.* Louisville: Westminster/John Knox, 1997.

Bauknight, Brian Kelly. *Body Building: Creating a Team Ministry Through Spiritual Gifts.* Nashville: Abingdon, 1996.

Becker, Palmer. *Called To Equip.* Scottsdale, Pa.: Herald Press, 1993.

Callahan, Kennon L. *Effective Church Leadership.* San Francisco: Harper & Row, 1990.

————. *Effective Church Leadership: Building on the Twelve Keys.* San Francisco: Jossey-Bass, 1997.

Clardis, George. *Leading the Team-Based Church.* San Francisco: Jossey-Bass, 1999.

Dale, Robert. *Leadership for a Changing Church: Charting the Shape of the River.* Nashville: Abingdon, 1998.

Gangel, Kenneth O. *Feeding and Leading: A Practical Handbook on Administration in Churches and Christian Organizations.* Wheaton, Ill.: Victor Books, 1989.

Henkelmann, Frank. *How to Develop a Team Ministry and Make it Work.* St. Louis: Concordia, 1985.

Hobgood, William Chris. *The Once and Future Pastor: The Changing Role of Religious Leaders.* Washington, D.C.: The Alban Institute, 1998.

Johnson, Douglas W. *Empowering Lay Volunteers.* Nashville: Abingdon, 1991.

Katzenbach, Jon R., and K. Douglas. *The Wisdom of Teams Creating the High-Performance Organization.* Boston: Harvard Business School Press, 1993.

Lewis, Philip V. *Transformational Leadership: A New Model for Total Church Involvement.* Nashville: Broadman & Holman, 1996.

McGinnis, Alan Loy. *Bringing Out the Best in People.* Minneapolis: Augsburg, 1985.

McIntosh, Gary L. *The Exodus Principle: A 5-Part Strategy to Free Your People for Ministry.* Nashville: Broadman & Holman, 1995.

McNeal, Reggie, ed. *Revolution in Leadership: Training Apostles for Tomorrow's Church.* Nashville: Abingdon, 1998.

Maddux, Robert B. *Delegating for Results.* Los Altos, Calif.: Crisp Publishing, 1990.

————. *Team Building: An Exercise in Leadership.* Los Altos, Calif.: Crisp Publications, 1988.

Maxwell, John. *Developing the Leader Within You.* Nashville: Thomas Nelson, 1993.

———. *Developing the Leaders Around You.* Nashville: Thomas Nelson, 1995.

Malphurs, Aubrey. *Developing a Vision for Ministry in the 21ST Century.* Grand Rapids: Baker Book House, 1992.

Miller, Herb. *The Vital Church Leader.* Nashville: Abingdon, 1991.

Nouwen, Henri J. M. *In the Name of Jesus: Reflections on Christian Leadership.* New York: Crossroad, 1996.

Page, Patricia N. *All God's People Are Ministers: Equipping Church Members for Ministry.* Minneapolis: Augsburg, 1993.

Schaller, Lyle E. *Create Your Own Future!* Nashville: Abingdon, 1991.

———. *Empowering Lay Volunteers: Creative Leadership Styles.* Nashville: Abingdon, 1991.

Shawchuck, Norman, and Roger Heuser. *Leading the Congregation.* Nashville: Abingdon, 1993.

Sofield, Loughlan, and Donald H. Kuhn. *The Collaborative Leader: Listening to the Wisdom of God's People.* Notre Dame, Ind.: Ave Maria Press, 1995.

Steinbron, Melvin J. *Can the Pastor Do It Alone?* Ventura, Calif.: Regal Books, 1987.

Trumbauer, Jean Morris. *Sharing the Ministry.* Minneapolis: Augsburg, 1995.

Van Auken, Philip. *The Well-Managed Ministry.* Wheaton, Ill.: Victor Books, 1989.

Weems, Lovett H., Jr. *Church Leadership: Vision, Team, Culture and Integrity.* Nashville: Abingdon, 1993.

Evangelism

Barna, George. *Marketing the Church.* Colorado Springs: NavPress, 1988.

Celek, Tim, Dieter Zander, and Patrick Kampert. *Inside the Soul of a New Generation: Insights and Strategies for Reaching Busters.* Grand Rapids: Zondervan, 1996.

Chaney, Charles L. *Church Planting at the End of the Twentieth Century.* Wheaton, Ill.: Tyndale House, 1991.

Dawn, Marva. *Reaching Out Without Dumbing Down.* Grand Rapids: Eerdmans, 1995.

Easum, William. *The Complete Ministry Audit: How to Measure 20 Principles for Growth.* Nashville: Abingdon, 1996.

———. *How to Reach Baby Boomers.* Nashville: Abingdon, 1991.

Easum, William, and Thomas Bandy. *Growing Spiritual Redwoods.* Nashville: Abingdon, 1997.

Faircloth, Samuel D. *Church Planting for Reproduction.* Grand Rapids: Baker Book House, 1991.

Finke, Roger, and Rodney Stark, *The Churching of America 1776–1990.* New Brunswick, N.J.: Rutgers University Press, 1992.

George, Carl. *Prepare Your Church for the Future.* New York: Revell, 1991.

Gibbs, Eddie. *In Name Only: Tackling the Problem of Nominal Christianity.* Wheaton, Ill.: Bridge Point Books, 1994.

Green, Michael. *Evangelism Through the Local Church*. Nashville: Thomas Nelson, 1992.

Hall, Douglas John. *Why Christian? For Those on the Edge of Faith*. Philadelphia: Fortress, 1998.

Henderson, D. Michael. *John Wesley's Class Meeting: A Model for Making Disciples*. Nappanee, Ind.: Evangel Publishing House, 1997.

Hunter, George G. *Church for the Unchurched*. Nashville: Abingdon, 1996.

———. *How to Reach Secular People*. Nashville: Abingdon, 1992.

Miller, Herb. *The Vital Congregation*. Nashville: Abingdon, 1990.

Rainer, Thom S. *Giant Awakenings: Making the Most of 9 Surprising Trends that Can Benefit Your Church*. Nashville: Broadman & Holman, 1994.

———. *High Expectations: The Remarkable Secret for Keeping People in Your Church*. Nashville: Broadman & Holman, 1994.

Roxburgh, Alan J. *Reaching a New Generation: Strategies for Tomorrow's Church*. Downer's Grove, Ill.: InterVarsity Press, 1993.

Sample, Tex. *U.S. Lifestyles and Mainline Churches*. Louisville: Westminster John Knox, 1990.

Scifres, Mary J. *Searching for Seekers: Ministry with a New Generation of the Unchurched*. Nashville: Abingdon, 1998.

Shawchuck, Norman et al. *Marketing for Congregations: Choosing to Serve People More Effectively*. Nashville: Abingdon, 1992.

Strobel, Lee. *Inside the Mind of Unchurched Harry and Mary*. Grand Rapids: Zondervan, 1993.

Seeker Services

Barna, George. *User Friendly Churches*. Ventura, Calif.: Regal Books, 1990.

Callahan, Kennon L. *Dynamic Worship: Mission, Grace, Praise, and Power: A Manual for Strengthening the Worship Life of Twelve Keys Congregations*. San Francisco: Jossey-Bass, 1997.

Dobson, Ed. *Starting a Seeker-Sensitive Service: How Traditional Churches Can Reach the Unchurched*. Grand Rapids: Zondervan, 1993.

Jones, Ezra Earl. *Quest for Quality in the Church: A New Paradigm*. Nashville: Discipleship Resources, 1993.

Owens, Bill. *The Magnetic Music Ministry*. Nashville: Abingdon, 1996.

Sample, Tex. *The Spectacle of Worship in a Wired World: Electronic Culture and the Gathered People of God*. Nashville: Abingdon, 1998.

Shawchuck, Norman, and Gustave J. Rath. *Benchmarks of Quality in the Church: 21 Ways to Continuously Improve the Content of Your Ministry*. Nashville: Abingdon, 1994.

Troeger, Thomas H. *Ten Strategies for Preaching in a Multimedia Culture*. Nashville: Abingdon, 1996.

Wright, Tim, and Jan Wright. *Contemporary Worship*. Nashville: Abingdon, 1997.

Mobilizing for Mission

Bartruff, Bryce Duane. *Here Am I Send Me: The Recruitment, Management, and Training of Volunteers*. Joplin, Mo.: College Press, 1992.

Bosch, David J. *Transforming Mission: Paradigm Shifts in the Field of Mission*. Maryknoll, N.Y.: Orbis, 1997.

Buford, Bob. *Half Time: Changing Your Game Plan from Success to Significance*. Grand Rapids: Zondervan, 1997.

Callahan, Kennon L. *Twelve Keys to an Effective Church: Strategic Planning for Mission*. San Francisco: Harper & Row, 1983.

Cook, Paul, and Judith Zeiler. *Neighborhood Ministry Basics: A No-Nonsense Guide*. Washington, D.C.: Pastoral Press, 1986.

Dudley, Carl. *Making the Small Church Effective*. Nashville: Abingdon, 1978.

Easum, William M. *Dancing with Dinosaurs: Ministry in a Hostile and Hurting World*. Nashville: Abingdon, 1993.

Edington, Howard, and Lyle E. Schaller. *Downtown Church: The Heart of the City*. Innovators in Ministry. Nashville: Abingdon, 1996.

Flynn, Anne E. *Dare to Believe, Dare to Act: A Parish Formation Program for Ministry and Service to Others*. Collegeville, Minn.: Liturgical Press, 1997.

Hershey, Terry, Karen Butler, and Rich Hurst. *Giving the Ministry Away*. Elgin, Ill.: David C. Cook, 1992.

Hunsberger, George, and Craig VanGelder, ed. *Church Between Gospel and Culture: The Emerging Mission in North America*. Grand Rapids: Eerdmans, 1996.

Menking, Stanley J. *Helping Laity Help Others*. Philadelphia: Westminster, 1984.

Morris, Margie. *Volunteer Ministries: New Strategies for Today's Church*. Sherman, TX: Newton-Cline Press, 1990.

Myers, Ched. *Who Will Roll Away the Stone?: Discipleship Queries for First World Christians*. Maryknoll, N.Y.: Orbis Books, 1994.

Steinbron, Melvin J. *The Lay-Driven Church*. Ventura, Calif.: Regal Books, 1997.

Stevens, Paul. *The Equipper's Guide to Every-Member Ministry: Eight Ways Ordinary People Can Do the Work of the Church*. Downers Grove, Ill.: InterVarsity Press, 1993.

———. *Equipping the Laity*. Downers Grove, Ill.: InterVarsity Press, 1993.

Stevens, Paul, and Phil Collins, *The Equipping Pastor: A Systems Approach to Congregational Leadership*. Bethesda, Md.: The Alban Institute, 1993.

Tillapaugh, Frank. *Unleashing the Church*. Ventura, Calif.: Regal Books, 1985.

Van Engen, Charles. *God's Missionary People: Rethinking the Purpose of the Local Church*. Grand Rapids: Baker Book House, 1991.

Vendura, Nancy. *Go Do the Same: Developing Parish Outreach Programs*. New York: Paulist, 1992.

Vineyard, Sue. *Evaluating Volunteers, Programs and Events*. Downers Grove, Ill.: Heritage Arts Publishing, 1988.

Welte, Jerry. *Ministry in a Messy World: A New Model for Effective Ministry*. San Jose, Calif.: Resource Publications, Inc., 1989.

Wendland, Barbara. *God's Partners: Lay Christians at Work*. Valley Forge, Pa.: Judson Press, 1993.

Williams, Dennis E., and Kenneth O Gangel. *Volunteers for Today's Church: How to Recruit and Retain Workers*. Grand Rapids: Baker Book House, 1993.

Wilson, Marlene. *How to Mobilize Church Volunteers*. Minneapolis: Augsburg, 1983.

Postmodern Resources for New Paradigm Churches

Anderson, Walt. *The Truth About the Truth: De-confusing and Re-constructing the Postmodern World (New Consciousness Reader)*. Los Angeles: Jeremy P. Tarcher, 1995.

Baker, Joel. *Future Edge*. New York: Morrow, 1992.

Barna, George. *Virtual American*. Ventura, Calif.: Regal Books, 1994.

Beaudoin, Tom. *Virtual Faith: The Irreverent Spiritual Quest of Generation X*. San Francisco: Jossey-Bass, 1998.

Cimino, Richard, and Don Lattin. *Shopping for Faith: American Religion in the New Millennium*. San Francisco: Jossey-Bass, 1998.

Drucker, Peter F. *The Age of Discontinuity: Guidelines to Our Changing Society*. New Brunswick, N.J.: Transaction Publishers, 1992.

———. *Landmarks of Tomorrow: A Report on the New 'Post-modern' World*. New Brunswick, N.J.: Transaction Publishers, 1996.

Drucker, Peter Ferdinand. *Management Challenges for the 21ST Century*. New York: Harperbusiness, 1999.

Easum, William. *Sacred Cows Make Gourmet Burgers*. Nashville: Abingdon, 1995.

Fields, Doug. *Purpose Driven Youth Ministry: 9 Essential Foundations for Healthy Growth*. Grand Rapids: Zondervan, 1998.

Grenz, Stanley J. *A Primer on Postmodernism*. Grand Rapids: Eerdmans, 1996.

Hybels, Bill, and Lynne Hybels. *Rediscovering Church: The Story and Vision of Willow Creek Community Church*. Grand Rapids: Zondervan, 1995.

Imparato, Nicholas. *Jumping the Curve*. San Francisco: Jossey-Bass, 1994.

Jones, Steven G. *Cybersociety: Computer-Mediated Communication and Community*. Thousand Oaks, Calif.: Sage Publications, 1995.

Kellner, Mark A. *God on the Internet*. Foster City, Calif.: IDG Books Worldwide, 1996.

Miller, Craig K. *Post-Moderns: The Beliefs, Hopes, and Fears of Young Americans*. Nashville: Discipleship Resources, 1996.

Nash, Robert. *An 8-Track Church in a CD World*. Macon, Ga.: Smyth & Helwys Publishing, 1998.

Popcorn, Faith, and Lys Marigold. *Clicking: 17 Trends That Drive Your Business—And Your Life*. New York: Harperbusiness, 1998.

Riddell, Michael. *Threshold of the Future: Reforming the Church in the Post-Christian West*. London: SPCK, 1998.

Sample, Tex. *The Spectacle of Worship in a Wired World: Electronic Culture and the Gathered People of God*. Nashville: Abingdon, 1998.

Slaughter, Michael. *Out on the Edge: A Wake-Up Call for Church Leaders on the Edge of the Media Reformation*. Nashville: Abingdon, 1998.

Sweet, Leonard I. *AquaChurch*. Loveland, Colo.: Group Publishing, 1999.

———. *11 Genetic Gateways to Spiritual Awakening*. Nashville: Abingdon, 1998.

———. *FaithQuakes*. Nashville: Abingdon, 1994.

————. *Quantum Spirituality.* Dayton, Ohio: United Theological Seminary, 1991.

————. *SoulTsunami.* Grand Rapids: Zondervan, 1999.

Turkle, Sherry. *Life on the Screen: Identity in the Age of the Internet.* New York: Simon and Schuster, 1995.

Veith, Gene Edward, Jr.. *Postmodern Times: A Christian Guide to Contemporary Thought and Culture.* Wheaton, Ill.: Crossway Books, 1994.

Warren, Rick. *The Purpose Driven Church: Growth Without Compromising Your Message & Mission.* Grand Rapids: Zondervan, 1995.

CONTRIBUTORS

Leonard Sweet is currently dean of the Theological School and vice president of Drew University. He is a popular speaker, futurist, church consultant, and author of many books on the ancient/future church, including the postmodern trilogy: *SoulTsunami, AquaChurch,* and *SoulSausa* (1999–2000).

The Reverend Jessica Farish Moffatt is senior pastor of First United Methodist Church of Bixby, Oklahoma, and a popular speaker. Prior to her current appointment she developed the Community Ministries program at First United Methodist Church in Tulsa, Oklahoma, where she also served as a commissioner on the mayor's appointed Commission on the Status of Women. With her background in international relations and the fine arts, Jessica speaks throughout the United States on how churches and businesses might improve their cities and strengthen their faith through community service.

Russell Moy, Ph.D., is assistant professor of Christian Education at the Church Divinity School of the Pacific and Graduate Theological Union, in Berkeley, California. While at Drew University, his courses on equipping laity for ministry were very popular among seminarians. Moy is an ordained American Baptist minister who affirms the priesthood of all believers. His gift for ministry (as well as his Ph.D. from Claremont School of Theology) is in the field of religious education.

Christine M. Anderson, M.A.T.S., M.B.A. is an active member of Willow Creek Community Church in South Barrington, Illinois, where she volunteers in Seeds, the church's bookstore; leads a service small group; and serves as a lay pastor in the church's Community Care ministry.

Christine works part-time as associate editor for *The Covenant Companion,* the denominational magazine of the Evangelical Covenant Church headquartered in Chicago, Illinois. She also enjoys freelance writing and editing, and once a week works a night shift as a chaplain at Swedish Covenant Hospital on Chicago's North Side. Previously, she held editorial and marketing positions at HarperSanFrancisco, a division of HarperCollins Publishers; and Zondervan Publishing House in Grand Rapids, Michigan.

Brian K. Bauknight, D.Min., has been the minister for preaching and oversight at Christ United Methodist Church in Bethel Park, Pennsylvania, since 1980. He is author of five books, including *Gracious Imperatives: Discipleship Toward the 21st Century* (Abingdon, 1992) and *Body Building: Creating a Ministry Team Through Spiritual Gifts* (Abingdon, 1996). He and his congregation and staff team provide leadership as a "teaching church" for the Larger Membership Church Initiative of The United Methodist Church. Brian also teaches an online Bible study and a continuing education Internet course for Drew Theological School.

The Reverend Eric Park serves as one of the pastors of Christ United Methodist Church in Bethel Park, Pennsylvania. His primary responsibility is to provide leadership and preaching for the church's four-year-old Sunday evening seeker-sensitive worship event. He is enrolled in the Global/Online Doctor of Ministry program at Drew University.

Robert J. Duncan Jr., D.Min., is director of Institutional Advancement and acting director of Theological Admissions at Drew Theological School. As a Dean's Fellow and charter participant in the Global/Online Doctor of Ministry program at Drew, his thesis included pioneer work on the "Electronification of the Church," and reinventing theological education using online learning. Duncan hosts and maintains *http://da.cihost.com/nextchurch*, a website devoted to interactive twenty-first-century ministry.

Michael J. Christensen, Ph.D., is director of the Doctor of Ministry Program at Drew Theological School and affiliate assistant professor of spirituality at the Graduate School of Drew University. Currently he is project manager and senior consultant of the psychosocial component of the Chernobyl Childhood Illness Recovery Project funded by the U.S. Agency for International Development. His training specialty is community mental health promotion utilizing indigenous leaders, organizational volunteers, and paraprofessionals. Dr. Christensen is the author of five books, including: *City Streets, City People: A Call to Compassion; The Samaritan's Imperative: Compassionate Ministry to People Living with AIDS;* and *Children of Chernobyl: Raising Hope from the Ashes.* He is general editor of *TheNextChurch* series published by Abingdon.

Carl E. Savage, D.Min., is associate director of the Doctor of Ministry Program and a Ph.D. candidate in New Testament and Early Christian Studies at Drew University. After pastoring for twenty years in the Virginia Conference of The United Methodist Church, Savage came to Drew and now coordinates the Global/Online Doctor of Ministry program.

He also is a director with the Bethsaida Excavations Project, an archaeological dig in Israel. He is the author of *What Does the Bible Mean?: Scripture Interpretation Through the Centuries* (Discipleship Resources, 1985) and serves as associate editor of *TheNextChurch* series.